D0016289

BASS MASTER SHAW GRIGSBY

Notes on Fishing and Life

BASS MASTER SHAW GRIGSBY

Notes on Fishing and Life

Shaw E. Grigsby, Jr.

with Robert Coram

National Geographic Books
Washington, D.C.

NATIONAL
GEOGRAPHIC
SOCIETY

Published by the National Geographic Society
1145 17th Street, N.W.
Washington, D.C. 20036

Library of Congress Cataloging-in-Publication Data

Grigsby, Shaw E.
     Bass master Shaw Grigsby : notes on fishing and life / Shaw E.
  Gigsby with Robert Coram.
       p. cm.
  ISBN 0-7922-7376-1
     1. Bass fishing. 2. Grigsby, Shaw E. I. Coram, Robert.
  II. Title.
  SH681.G74 1998   98-30572
  799.1'773—dc21   CIP

First printing, October 1998
Printed in the United States of America

Art by Jack Unruh

For Dad,
who taught me a love of the outdoors
and gave me lessons for life.

CONTENTS

~

THE BASS

~

I am a bass fisherman.

I have fished for muskie in Lake St. Clair and for tarpon in the Gulf of Mexico. I have fished for panfish in little ponds and for amberjack off the Islamorada Hump. I have fished for barracuda in the Florida Keys and for king salmon in Alaska. I have fished in 36 states and 4 foreign countries for virtually every freshwater and saltwater game fish known to man. I have fished in tournaments since I was 16 and have been a professional angler for almost two decades. And I can tell you that there is no fish anywhere in the world to equal the bass.

I have won five major tournaments and fished the BASS Masters Classic eight times. I am in the all-time five top money winners among professional bass anglers. But I remain a mystified amateur when it comes to figuring out and understanding the bass.

Countless times I have been fishing when the sun came up and was still fishing when it went down. I have fished the still and quiet white-hot days of summer, and I have fished in winter—in the sleet and snow and when the wind howled and the waves tossed the boat like a toy, and when it was so cold that I shivered under five layers of clothing and wondered if I would ever again be warm. I have competed in hundred-thousand-dollar tournaments and won more than a million dollars as a professional angler.

I have also been skunked.

I am middle-aged now and my experiences as a professional

angler, like my memories, are rich and continue to grow. One day I shall be old and there will be many stories to tell my grandchildren. The one they will hear most often, the one that will cause them to smile every time I begin, will be of the day I caught my first bass.

It was midmorning on a fine summer day and I was five years old. My dad and my uncle and I were in Louisiana fishing the Little River, a slow-moving, muddy river about 50 yards wide and filled with sticks, limbs, and logs. Dad and my uncle were out in a boat fishing a laydown, a tree that had fallen into the water and formed the kind of shelter so loved by bass. I was on the bank fishing with a little Zebco 33 reel and throwing an H&H spinner, a spinner bait with two blades and a double hook. I was casting and reeling, casting and reeling, watching my dad out in the boat.

I threw out the bait and started to retrieve it when suddenly it stopped. *The bait has snagged a log*, I thought, *and I'm going to have to wade out and get it.*

Then all at once it took off.

Ziiiiiinnnnnggg!

"Dad! Dad!" I screamed. I was cranking away but not gaining. The fish was taking drag. Dad turned around in the boat to watch.

This was the biggest fish I had ever caught, and I was so afraid it would get away. I turned, put the rod over my shoulder, and ran up the bank—and kept running until I dragged the fish out of the water. Then I ran a few more steps. The fish hit the mudbank and was flopping all over the place. Now I was afraid he would flop back into the river. I dropped the rod, ran back, and threw myself on top of him. He weighed about 3½ pounds. He was a good bass.

My dad came to the bank and helped me stringer the fish. He was so proud of me. He was laughing. I had caught a few bluegills before, but bass were special critters—what the grown-ups caught. I was strutting around with a grown-up fish.

I had caught a bass.

But it was I who was hooked.

Much of what we Americans know about fishing, we learned from the English. The lean and elegant trout and the robust salmon were their fish of choice. And for generations those were the fish prized by American anglers.

But sometime around the turn of the century, the black bass began making his presence known, first across the rural South as a plentiful food fish and then as a wily sport fish.

The bass is an American fish. It ranges from Canada to Mexico and from the Atlantic to the Pacific. Every state but Alaska has a bass population. The bass inhabits thousands of small ponds, natural lakes, impoundments, rivers, and tidal waters. And while bass fishing is still thought of as a southern sport, some of the best bass waters in America are in the north country: in New York, Vermont, Minnesota, and along the Canadian border.

The largemouth is the best known of all bass, and the largest member of the sunfish family, which includes bluegills, bream, crappies, and perch among others. There is also the smallmouth, which does not like warm southern waters and is found roughly from the middle tier states to the Canadian border. The smallmouth, which we call "browny" or "smallie," is not as big as the largemouth. It has a brownish cast, while the largemouth is olive green.

While the largemouth is native to American waters, he has become so prized as a game fish in other parts of the world that we have exported him to dozens of countries, and today he reigns in countries as far apart as Japan and South Africa, as Italy and Zimbabwe.

The largemouth is a fish truly worthy of admiration.

Perhaps one in a thousand reaches maturity. From the moment he hatches, the fry draws the attention of predators.

As the fry becomes a minnow, he is preyed upon by herons. When he is grown, cormorants, ospreys, eagles, otters, alligators, and finally, fishermen pursue him.

The bass will continue to grow throughout their lifetime. And once his survival instincts are fully developed, he looks around his world with the confidence of a shark. He reigns as the king daddy of predators.

The lower jaw juts forth and slopes back and down so that even when he is resting he has a bold, aggressive look. His mouth opens to an enormous circle far out of proportion to the size of his body—so big you can look down it and see his gizzards. His mouth gives him his nicknames of Big Mouth or Bucket Lips. His shape gives him his nicknames of Hawg, Lunker, or Sow. And his disposition gives him the simple and always respectful nickname of Mr. Bass. He is big, broad shouldered and heavyset; a swaggering redneck linebacker of a fish. He has two dorsal fins; the first has ten spikes and gives him the appearance of a prehistoric creature. He is primitive, powerful, belligerent, and unpredictable. He is prone to random acts of violence.

It is good that God did not allow him to grow any bigger. If he weighed 60 or 70 pounds, the waters of America would not be safe for swimming.

His survival instinct is even better developed than his muscles. He is very, very savvy about what is going on around him.

Bass have the best and most adaptable camouflage of any creature in nature. You've heard that the leopard can't change its spots? Well, the bass can. He has color cells that enable him to do just that. If he's lurking in a patch of grass, he can darken his olive green topside until he is almost black. If he passes over a sandy bottom, he can lighten his coloration until he is virtually invisible to the angler.

Bass are sometimes found in schools. If you see shad breaking the surface of the water, twirling and dancing like silver dollars flung across a sheet of tin, you know a school of bass is on the move.

Then there are the individual bass—the loners, the hermits. These solitary fish are territorial and moody and quick to anger. They hide in shadowy underwater hydrilla beds or around fallen brush piles and trees, places as dim as medieval cathedrals, because they do not want to chase their dinner. They lurk, knowing dinner will come to them. And when their prey swims a few inches away, they explode. Then they return, sole dwellers of their cathedrals, until another meal passes by.

The bass has been written about as much as any fish in the world. More than 4,000 outdoor writers regularly turn out stories and columns, the content of which generally runs to tips, advice, and instructions on how to catch the bass. Folklore about bass fishing is passed down through generations. Many states have fisheries experts who do nothing but study the bass. American industry and American anglers spend 41 billion dollars a year on technology, magic lures, and boats, all aimed at helping the angler gain an advantage over the bass. The body of information about this one fish is truly astonishing.

Yet we know so little.

We can make broad guesses about what the bass will do or where he will be based on food or structure or water temperature or weather or seasonal migration patterns or type of lake or depth of water. But when you get right down to it, that's all they are. Guesses.

For years we have mounted the equivalent of a major military operation against a single species of fish—a fish that fisheries experts say is not very smart. Yet he is smart enough that we can't always catch him.

The largemouth bass, *Micropterus salmoides*, is the most hunted freshwater fish in the world; America alone has more than 31 million bass fishermen. Put another way, 40 percent of all freshwater anglers are bass fishermen—that's almost 7 percent of the U.S. population older than 16.

If you look at the bass objectively, it is difficult to figure out why he is the king of the freshwater sport fish. Other fish are more aggressive. Other fish are bigger. Other fish are easier to catch and taste better. Other fish are more elegant. Other fish offer a more contemplative challenge to the angler.

Maybe it's because the bass wins as often as the fisherman. No one can figure out the bass completely.

The best bass fishermen are metaphysical in their ability to enter nature and to think like a bass, to almost become a bass as they consider the habitat, the food, all the needs and concerns of the fish.

Any fisherman can catch fish when the fish are hungry. But a good bass fisherman can coax a fish to strike when it is not hungry.

The bass strikes a lure for many reasons. Sometimes he is saying, "Get out of here." He will strike because he is territorial; it's his version of throwing a salesman away from the front door or hanging up on a telemarketer. Sometimes he strikes before he thinks, simply out of reaction. He could be hovering, half asleep, and you put a plug in front of him ten times. He ignores every cast. Then, on the eleventh cast, he decides he has had enough and thumps it good: He eats it—simply because he doesn't like the noise it makes.

Much of bass fishing is taunting the fish, trying to make him angry enough to strike.

People say that golf is a very complex game, and there is a lot more to playing golf than hitting a little ball across neatly mowed grass into a hole in the ground. I can tell you there is a whole lot more to bass fishing than casting a bait and retrieving it.

People who play golf talk about how complex and sophisticated it is. Golf has the reputation of being the most cerebral of all professional sports. But it is not. The most complex, most sophisticated and cerebral of all professional sports is bass fishing.

The most obvious difference is that when you pursue the bass, you pursue not a little ball but a living creature with a highly developed sense of survival—a creature that moves and thinks and remembers and reacts.

Before you can catch him, you must find him. And find him under conditions that can change from minute to minute. Consider the variables. Most of the time you can't see him. He can be in 6 inches of water or 30 feet down, or any depth in between. He can be basking on the surface, lurking behind a stump, or hiding in deep grass. He can be at the mouth of a creek or on a rocky point—a piece of land that juts into a river or lake (Bass love points).

He can be anywhere.

And something as uncontrollable as the sun going behind a cloud or an unexpected wind that ruffles the surface can cause him to move in an instant.

Once we find him—if we find him—we must entice him to bite.

Most fish bite because they are hungry: Figure out what they are eating, and you'll catch them. That's how trout guides make their living. But it's not that way with bass. I have caught a bass, opened his mouth, and seen the tail of another fish. He was so full he was bloated. But he still took the bait.

The bass will strike out of anger, aggression, reaction, or territoriality.

Some days he won't strike no matter what you offer him. Other days he is so aggressive, he'll leap out of the water and gulp the bait while it's still in the air.

The Holy Grail of bass fishing is the search for the magic bait, for the lure that the bass will strike under all conditions. Large companies spend fortunes developing new baits. And numerous professional anglers put their names and reputations on new baits that they want to promote.

But no one has found the magic bait and I don't think they ever will.

It may sound like a contradiction to what I have just said, but if you are fishing for bass and not catching them, you are doing something wrong. You are not thinking like a bass. You are not in tune with his survival instinct, his territoriality. You are not understanding what is going on in the world of Mr. Bass.

I have fished for the bass in ponds, lakes, impoundments, rivers, and tidal waters. And I have learned much that will benefit both the beginning and the experienced angler.

In this book I want to show you how to eliminate variables and how to catch bass any time of the day, under all conditions. I want to teach you how to catch bass not only in your home waters but in any waters. I want to show you how to go from the civilized world to the wild world; how to enter the world of the bass—how to move in that world and be at one with that world.

To go into strange waters and consistently catch bass is proof that you have crossed from your world into the world of a wild creature. You have crossed the line. You have pierced the veil. You have entered another dimension.

This is what you must do if you are to prevail against the bass. If you think this is mystical nonsense, you will never become a first-rate fisherman.

Those of us who are professional bass anglers hold many secrets in our hearts. Some we would not even share with our wives or sons, much less another fisherman.

But in this book I will share my secrets; I will tell you how I find bass and how I catch them. And I will share my observations and give you tips, all that I have learned during nearly three decades of bass fishing. I do not say that reading this book will guarantee that every time you go on the water you'll catch a limit—that you'll go to weigh-in with a big smile because you caught the tournament's maximum number allowed. If bass fishermen were always successful, the bass would be an endangered species. But the bass lives and thrives and wins more often than he loses.

If you are a bass fisherman, you already know that.

You know that bass fishing is the most complicated and challenging of all professional sports.

BEGINNINGS

~

The Waccasassa River is about an hour west of Gainesville. It is a small river about 80 feet across and, like many of Florida's rivers, filled with tannic acid, which makes it the color of weak tea. The river is slow-moving, bordered by overhanging cypress trees, and, beyond the sandy banks, by tall pines. South of Cedar Key, as the river approaches the Gulf of Mexico, the Waccasassa fans into a large marsh and then into dozens of small fingers that reach for the great expanse of the Gulf.

My family used to go there often in the winter to fish for red fish. Dad always brought his 5hp motor. We would go to the fish camp at Waccasassa, rent a 14-foot boat, put dad's outboard on it, and off we'd go. We fished the little fingers and around the numerous oyster bars. The river could be confusing there because it was shallow and there were no channel markers.

We always kept a weather eye toward the Gulf, watching for the winter fronts that occasionally roared through.

The little rental boat was flat-bottomed with a V-bow and maybe a two-foot deck at the bow. We kept a thermos of hot chocolate under the little deck. All of us would bundle up under big coats. My sister and I were dwarfed in them. We'd drink hot chocolate and snuggle up with mom while dad fished. The boat had a hand tiller, and sometimes dad let me steer.

We putted around, waiting in the creek mouths for the tide to fall. Red fish go up the creeks on a high tide, and as the tide ebbed, we could see the fish washing across the oyster bars. We always carried extra shear pins for the propeller because dad sometimes hit an oyster bar.

Dad was a fish-catching machine.

We couldn't stringer the fish in saltwater because the sharks would eat them, so we put them in a cooler and took them home and ate them.

In the summers we went up to Highlands, North Carolina, where we camped and fished for trout. We had a little camping stove that mom cooked the fish on. She cooked them in butter. We ate trout for breakfast, lunch, and dinner.

Sometimes I got up at daylight and caught fish for breakfast. My jeans would be icy and stiff from the previous day; putting them on was enough to wake me up. Then I'd step into the cold mountain stream and shuffle across the rocks to good water. I was cold and wet. But when the first bite came around sunup, it made everything worthwhile. I forgot the discomfort.

I don't know a better way to start the day than by catching a trout as the sun comes up.

It was in North Carolina that I learned to use a spinning rod. And it was in North Carolina that I first began to learn about the habits of fish. I saw how trout related to cover and structure. I saw how they related to rocks, how they positioned themselves in an eddy, how they utilized the flow of the current to set up an ambush. Knowing the habits of trout was of great benefit when I began observing bass.

Many evenings in our home we sat around listening to the radio; that was in the sixties, before we had a television. Dad smoked and tinkered with his tackle. He had tackle boxes full of stuff. Just stuff. Dad made many of his own baits. He took great pride in making baits and catching fish with them. He said if you make a bait, you are doing something to entice the fish. You're being much more personal with Mr. Bass.

From the very beginning, my dad implanted in the marrow of my bones, at the core of my being, a love of the outdoors. It was from my dad that I first heard the beckoning of the waters.

Any story about a bass fisherman must begin with his dad.

My dad was about five feet six inches tall and of slender build. He usually wore khaki shirts and khaki pants and often had a cigarette in his mouth. After he finished college, he joined the Navy and was an observer at the Bikini atomic bomb tests. After one of the tests, he jumped into the water to pick up a drifting buoy that, as it turned out, was so hot from radiation that he was sent to the Navy hospital at Bethesda, Maryland, for a month. Doctors there said he would never have children.

After World War II, he worked for the State Department and was assigned to Germany, where he studied how bombed-out cities could be rebuilt. He met Sigrid Werner. She became his wife. Then my older sister and I came along and proved the doctors wrong.

While I was growing up, my dad was a professor at the University of Florida in Gainesville. But I remember him mostly as an outdoorsman, a hunter and fisherman who took our family into the wilderness on many weekends and on many vacations.

Once we spent our vacation traveling out West, camping every night from Gainesville to Yellowstone and through the Grand Tetons.

We were Team Grigsby; we did it all together.

My mom tells me that my age was still measured by months when dad wrapped me up and placed me in a basket in the bow of a small boat and took me fishing. I was rocked by the waters from an early age.

I was so young when I caught my first bluegill that I don't even remember it.

Many of my early memories revolve around fishing.

THE BASS ANGLER

~

Fishing is both an escape from the busy world and a reconnection with the past.

For anyone whose life is filled with his work, fishing is a way of relaxing, maybe with a big cigar and a cold beer. Every time this person catches a fish, he knows he has fooled a living creature into taking the bait. He enjoys the pursuit of the fish—the escape from the world.

Some fishermen, usually those who go after panfish or catfish, take their catch home. They are putting food on the table. For them, fishing is a reconnection with the past.

There are certain generalizations you can make about fishermen based on the fish that is being pursued.

Saltwater fishermen generally are wealthier. They run to the liberal side and like to party. The fun side of fishing appeals to them.

Trout fishermen dress in little vests and hats and are as much interested in the pursuit of the fish as in catching it. They enjoy the relaxation of being outdoors.

Then there are the bass fishermen, an odd and sometimes confusing philosophical mix. More often than not the bass angler is relatively conservative, openly religious, and has strong family values. Often his wife and children accompany him when he goes fishing.

The confusing philosophical mix is seen on environmental and conservation issues. Even though the bass fisherman is, in general, politically conservative, on conservation and environmental issues he is…well, I don't want to use the world militant, because of the images it brings up, but he is a very outspoken conservationist.

From the beginning, conservation has been a fundamental part of the Bass Anglers Sportsman Society (B.A.S.S.), the oldest and most prestigious organization of bass anglers. When Ray Scott formed the group he adopted ten goals, five of which concerned conservation of natural resources. Those goals were established before the Clean Water, Clean Air, and Endangered Species acts were passed by Congress.

B.A.S.S. once sued more than 200 Alabama corporations, charging them with pollution. And when the Tennessee Valley Authority (TVA) virtually destroyed bass fishing in Tennessee lakes by using an herbicide to kill grass, a prime bass habitat, more than 500 bass fishermen, pulling bass boats, staged one of the biggest parades ever held in Tennessee. It was billed as a funeral for the dead lakes, and it drew such publicity that TVA stopped using herbicides.

Ray Scott has publicly said that the aggressive environmental stands his organization took were a major impetus behind the creation in 1970 of the Environmental Protection Agency.

B.A.S.S. founded the Natural Resource Summit of America, a coalition designed as a national voice on environmental issues. And B.A.S.S. played a major role in passing the Wallop-Breaux bill, congressional legislation that annually returns about 150 million dollars to state fisheries.

But perhaps the best-known and most far-reaching of all the B.A.S.S. environmental programs is the catch-and-release program. Since 1971, almost every fish caught in a B.A.S.S. tournament has been released back into the waters from which it was caught.

B.A.S.S. made this practice almost universal. Even saltwater fishermen have adopted a version called tag-and-release.

Back in the fifties and early sixties, bass fishermen came off the water with big stringers of fish. Today that sight would be repugnant. I don't know a professional bass angler who takes his catch home.

We make our living catching bass, and we know that by releasing them we can catch them for years to come. During practice days, we release fish immediately. At tournaments, they are placed in aerated live wells, taken to weigh-in, then kept in aerated tanks with water that contains chemicals to replenish the slime coat and to treat any minor scrapes the fish might have sustained. Then he is released. More than 97 percent of the bass caught in B.A.S.S. tournaments are returned alive to the waters from whence they came.

Any angler who comes to weigh-in with a dead fish is penalized four ounces.

Maybe you don't think four ounces is much. But it was enough to cost Dalton Bobo the BASS Masters Classic in 1997. The Classic is the world series of bass fishing. Dalton Bobo came to weigh-in with a dead fish and, after the four-ounce penalty was applied, came in second by one ounce.

The Classic pays $100,000 in prize money and is said to be worth a million dollars in endorsements and sponsor benefits.

So that one dead bass cost Dalton Bobo a million dollars.

Maybe we are militant.

*"Shaw and I drew each other in
an invitational tournament on Lake Eufaula.
When he said he knew where the fish were,
I said, "Let's go." In a few hours both of us had
four fish. I lost one fish because I was using
10-pound test. Shaw was using 15-pound test
and bringing them to the boat, even through
heavy obstacles. Earlier Shaw had seen a
five-pounder in a ditch. We went after her.
It turned out there was an eight-pounder in the
ditch also. I made the first cast and missed
the eight-pounder. Then Shaw made a cast and
caught the five-pounder—and had his limit of
keepers. He held the branch of a tree and
positioned the boat so I could get a good cast,
then he handed me his rod with the
15-pound test on it. I've been fishing
24 years and no other angler has ever done
that for me. He gave me his fishing rod
knowing I was about to catch an
eight-pounder. He is a great individual."*

—Gary Klein

THREE THINGS TO KNOW

~

A bass fisherman needs to know three things.

Food.

Temperature.

Structure.

They are all connected.

The number one concern for the bass is food. So in the winter, when baitfish are in the deeper, warmer waters, the bass go deep. Look for them in the main channel, in creek channels, and along deep ledges.

In the spring, bass go shallow to spawn.

When fish are shallow, they are far more accessible to the fisherman. It takes less time for the bait to sink, and the fish don't have as much water to move around in.

Come summer, the fish move deep again, to the ledges and drops, maybe as deep as 30 feet.

In the fall, bass follow the baitfish migration into pockets and creeks, where they congregate until a cold front hits. Most bass are shallow or mid-depth as they chase food.

These are the basic migrations of the bass.

A bass, being cold-blooded, has a comfort zone. When he is in his comfort zone, he is most likely to strike. Cold water makes the bass sluggish and lethargic. It dulls his appetite. The best comfort zone for largemouth bass is when the water temperature ranges from the 60s to the 80s.

You can catch bass when the temperature is in the 40s and 50s, and you can catch them when the temperature is in the 80s and 90s. But they like the midrange best.

Structure and cover are words that some anglers use interchangeably. But I consider structure to be anything that changes the natural shape of the bottom of a lake or river—ledges, drop-offs, creek channels, or old roadbeds. Cover is bushes, logs, grass beds—any place where the bass can hide.

Bass use structure and cover to hide from anglers as well as prey. Bass are predators. But they don't like to chase food halfway across a lake. They want to jump out and attack, explode onto their prey, eat it, and go back to their ambush point. Back to their cover.

When you fish for the bass, think first of what he needs for food.

Then of the water temperature.

And finally what sort of structure he has available.

Rick Clunn understands all this better than any other fisherman I know. When he is on the fish, few can compete with him. He is a tremendous angler. I am in awe of how good he is.

He understands food, temperature, structure.

WATER

~

There are four basic types of water for a bass angler: ponds or natural lakes, reservoirs, rivers, and tidal rivers.

A pond or a natural lake has little or no current. A reservoir has current only if the floodgates are open and power is being generated.

A river has current.

A tidal river has a current that flows upstream as well as downstream.

And current makes a big difference.

Let's start with ponds.

It is in small ponds that many boys first fish for bass. The boys get permission from the owner, walk to the edge of the water, and have their beginnings as fishermen.

A pond is the perfect place to begin an education about bass. Ponds are special because there are so few variables. There is visible cover and invisible cover. Distances are short. There are not many places for a bass to hide. It is easy to fish all the habitats in a short period. A person can quickly figure out why he caught a fish or why he didn't catch a fish. A pond is easy to understand.

Here's how to fish a pond.

Figure out what you have in the pond. Look for the visible cover—where bass hide; then look for underwater structure. Work the cover.

Throw the bait into the middle of the pond and count how long it takes to reach the bottom. Then throw it ten feet to the right and see how long it takes. If you get a longer count, you know there is a drop-off; a shorter count, and you know the water is shallower. Concentrate on how the bottom feels when you drag a bait across it. Determine if the bottom has grass that can hold fish. Does it have tree stumps or rocks?

Take whatever bite you get and, based on what the bass are doing, develop a pattern: Were the fish caught in visual cover? Did they hit a moving bait or did they wait until it was still? Were the bites in the grass or up under the trees?

Don't use a crank bait on a new pond until you know what the bottom is like. The crank bait has treble hooks and is easy to snag. It costs about five dollars, so you don't want to lose it. In a new pond, try a plastic worm. If you lose a plastic worm, it doesn't cost much.

There is no better place to learn to fish for bass than in a pond. A pond is the elementary school for the education of a bass angler.

Now for lakes.

Some fishermen think it's a big jump from a pond to a lake. But lakes are essentially big ponds and are fished the same way.

The truly big jump is from a pond or lake to a reservoir. The amount of water can be daunting.

But Gary Klein taught me that if a fisherman can fish a pond or lake, he can fish a reservoir.

Gary says when a fisherman goes to a new reservoir, he should take a small section of water, maybe a creek or a cove—any area that can be fished in a day—and figure out the primary points and secondary points, structure, and cover. In other words, check out the land points projecting into the water; the creek channels and back of the creek; the visual cover and invisible underwater cover.

Don't worry about anything except that small section of water. Pretend that the small section is a pond or lake. Analyze the water. Look at all the details.

Think of the time of the year and the type of water, then fish your strengths.

Let the fish tell you what they want.

Did you get a bite on a point? Was it a primary point or a secondary point? Remember every bite.

Eliminate water as you fish the small section.

Develop a pattern. You can do all this in one day.

On the second day, utilize what you have learned and fish the reservoir.

Gary says an angler should fish his strengths on new water, not what he thinks he has to fish. Do your own thing. If you are good at fishing plastic worms, fish plastic worms. If you're a spinner-bait man, fish a spinner bait.

This thoughtful methodical approach beats jumping in your boat and running and gunning for ten hours.

This is the professional way to approach a reservoir.

Now for rivers.

The first fishing trip on a river can be intimidating.

An angler must understand the current in a river before he can understand the fish in a river.

Current sets up, or positions, bass in certain areas. The bass faces into the current from a place where he can ambush bugs, frogs, or catch baitfish.

The big problem is figuring out where the bass will set up.

Eddies are favorite places. This is a spot where the current breaks or slows as it reverses direction. Here fish can set up without effort. An eddy is a good ambush spot.

Some eddies are formed by an invisible underwater structure. Others are formed by trees than have fallen into the water. Behind each log or limb is an eddy. Eddies are also formed by big rocks.

Look for whatever breaks the current. Look for points, weirs, jetties, bridges, and pilings.

Many rivers have oxbow lakes or backwaters where the current slows or even stops. These are key areas for a bass angler.

When fishing rivers, we look for these areas.

Now for tidal rivers.

The main thing to remember about tidal rivers is that the bass repositions frequently. He repositions according to depth and according to current.

As the depth changes, the places where the fish are holding changes. On a falling tide, the decreasing depth causes the fish to reposition.

If you are fishing one side of a point on a falling tide, that spot will no longer be good on a rising tide. Check the other side of the point. Think like a bass and remember how he likes to position in the current. Eddies will be formed in different places when the current reverses.

When fishing tidal rivers, you will find a certain amount of predictability in the bass. If you caught fish on the north side of a point during a falling tide, go back to that spot during the next falling tide.

When I'm fishing a tidal river, the last two hours of a falling tide and the first two hours of a rising tide are my favorite times.

There is still another facet to fishing tidal rivers: saltwater. Saltwater fish mix with freshwater fish in tidal rivers. You spend as much time trying not to catch red fish or stripers as you do trying to catch bass.

Tidal rivers are wonderful. They are fun to fish.

TACKLE

~

I was fishing a tournament on the Neuse River and was up high in the standings. I was trying to concentrate on my fishing, which was hard to do because four or five competitors were fishing in the same area.

Just as I hooked a good fish, one of the amateur fishermen in the back of a competitor's boat shouted, "What kind of rod are you using? A seven-footer?"

"No. Six and a half feet, medium action," I answered.

He kept asking questions, and before I realized, it I had an on-the-water seminar going about tackle.

Deciding what tackle to buy is the first big decision facing a beginning angler. So many choices are available and so many people have so many different opinions on the subject.

Few aspects of bass fishing are written about as often or in such detail as the proper tackle. But this is a topic that consumes the angler. Every time I conduct a seminar, there are questions about tackle.

So let's tackle this question of tackle early on.

This is such a fundamental part of fishing that it should be resolved early in an angler's career. He must get past his concern about tackle before he can progress. He can't be out on the water wondering if he should be using a 6½-foot rod instead a 7-foot rod. He can't be wondering if he should be using fiberglass instead of graphite. He can't be wondering if he has the right reel for the type of fishing he's doing, or if he's got the right hook for whatever conditions he's experiencing.

When the angler goes on the water, he should not be thinking about tackle.

He should be thinking about the bass.

Where is the bass? What is the bass doing? What is the bass eating?

Tackle is not a subject that calls for deep thinking. It is simple, far simpler than most fishermen want to make it.

If the rod is comfortable in the angler's hand, if he likes it, then he has the proper rod.

Same with the reel.

It doesn't matter what tackle I use or what any other professional angler uses. What is important is what works best for you.

Some pros use a 6½-foot rod. Others a 7. But Hank Parker uses a 5½-foot rod with a pistol grip, and he is one of the all-time great spinner-bait fishermen.

The proper tackle is whatever feels comfortable to you.

Make your decision, then move on to become a better angler.

TIP

~

If a bass nips at your bait and either misses or doesn't take it, throw again on the same spot.

Anglers throw some pretty gaudy things in the water when they're trying to catch fish. And the bass bites a surprisingly large number. Bass come to a bait wanting to eat it. So if the bass struck your bait and missed, he may still be there and still looking. He doesn't know what happened. One minute he was about to have lunch, and the next minute there was nothing. So he is circling and wondering where his lunch went.

Throw again and you have a good chance of catching him.

TEXAS AND CAROLINA

~

Every beginning bass angler should learn the Texas rig and the Carolina rig.

The Texas rig is the standard rig for fishing plastic worms, lizards, or crawfish.

It's simple. A bullet weight—the standard is three-sixteenths, or a quarter of an ounce—is attached to the line against the head of the bait. It can slide or it can be pegged: slide if you are in open water, pegged if you are fishing cover.

A Texas rig is streamlined. It fishes through cover easily. It is a good rig that puts the bait on the bottom.

The Carolina rig separates the bait from the weight. When Carolina rigging, we generally use a three-quarters of an ounce weight. Maybe even an ounce. Below the weight is a glass or plastic bead and then a swivel. Between the swivel and the hook is a leader. Three feet is the standard length, although it can be as short as 18 inches or as long as 6 feet.

I use 20-pound test line on my reel with a 14-pound test leader. I prefer a green leader because it can't be seen underwater.

On the end is a 3/0 HP hook and the bait.

The Carolina rig has several advantages.

The heavy weight allows you to cast the bait a long distance and to present it to fish that might spook if you were closer, especially in clear water.

The weight also carries the bait to the bottom quickly. But since the weight lands first, the bait has a natural and subtle fall to the bottom, which is very effective at enticing spooked or tentative fish.

If you are fishing heavy cover and the bait is snagged, it is the lighter and shorter leader that breaks. You lose only a few feet of line and the hook, not the weight and swivel.

The Carolina rig is most commonly used in deep water to fish stumps, drop-offs, and creek channels. But you can fish it shallow. I've used it in three feet of water.

Carolina rigging is a way to both find fish and to go after the fish that you know are there.

BAITS

~

Bass anglers are always searching for the magic lure.

They have their choice of thousands of baits to put on the end of the line: Little ones, big ones, hundreds of colors, lengths, and hook options. Plastic worms, jigs, crank baits, top-water baits, jerk baits, and buzz baits.

It is easy for an angler to be overwhelmed.

Again and again, every pro is asked one question: When fishing is tough, when it is hard to figure out a pattern, when the bass won't bite, what bait do you use?

Anglers want to know what will catch bass when nothing else works.

In my boat I have 16 tackle boxes filled with baits—almost $10,000 worth of lures.

But a fisherman always has a primary bait, a confidence

bait; one that he knows will catch fish.

Some fishermen prefer a jig. Others, a worm.

For me it is the spinner bait. I put on a spinner bait and fish year-round, hot weather and cold. I fish it deep and fish it shallow. I fish it in trees, brush, and weeds.

It is my confidence bait.

When nothing else works, I haul out the spinner bait.

But fishermen should know that the bait is not what counts the most.

It is the fisherman.

At a tournament on Buggs Island, on the Virginia–North Carolina border, I made up two spinner baits to use on practice days.

Then I made three more for the tournament.

All five were identical: same heads, same blades, same skirts.

I fished them all and caught enough fish to place third in the tournament.

I put the baits back in my tackle box and didn't use them again until I was on Logan Martin in Alabama practicing for the Classic.

By the end of the first hour of fishing, I had broken all five baits.

That's how close I was to losing a lot of money at Buggs Island.

Titanium spinner baits are being made today that will flex and bend and won't break, and can be used again and again. But they may be too expensive for many anglers.

If you are in a tournament and catch a good stringer of bass on a regular spinner bait, don't use that bait again in competition.

You could lose a big fish.

And a tournament.

Some baits, a very few, are so good at catching fish that their commercial name becomes the generic name.

A soft-jerk bait, for instance, is usually called a Slug-O because that was the name of the first one.

A lipless crank bait is usually called a Rat-L-Trap because that is the commercial name for the most popular bait of this type.

The lipless crank bait is one of the best all-around baits. You will not find a bass angler's tackle box anywhere that doesn't contain a lipless crank bait. Or you shouldn't. A lipless crank bait is about as close to being a bass magnet as any bait can be.

The Rat-L-Trap is loaded up with noisemakers that the bass homes in on.

That's because bass are curious.

I have a friend who is a scuba diver. He was working underwater, hammering down big pieces of matting to prevent the growth of vegetation in a marina. He was swinging a big hammer underwater. He felt eyes on him. He turned around, and there hovering over his shoulder were 15 or 20 big bass. They wanted to know what was making the noise.

Bass are very curious.

The Rat-L-Trap works on that curiosity.

You can modify the lipless crank bait for deep water.

Here's how.

Use a quarter-inch drill bit to drill a hole in the head of the bait. Drill between the line tie and the nose.

The bait is hollow, so you only have to drill through the plastic. Then take a piece of soldering wire and push it into the drilled hole. Position it to block the space between the line tie and the front hook. This seals the cavity behind the head.

With vice grips, seize the bait and place it in a container of ice water. Angle it so that the bait is submerged except for the area where the hole is drilled.

Then put a couple of lead bullet weights in an old spoon. Hold the spoon over the eye of a gas stove or heat it with a propane torch. Wear a glove and safety glasses.

When the lead is melted, very carefully pour it into the hole in the bait. Pour until the hole overflows.

The ice water bath prevents the plastic bait from melting.

When the lead cools, whittle off the overflow, smooth it, then cover it with epoxy and repaint it.

Now you have a bait that will dive for deep water, stay deep, and remain stable in strong currents.

Most pro anglers have weighted lipless crank baits in their tackle boxes.

You can buy half a dozen crank baits of the same type, color, size, and model—from the same manufacturer—and there will be vast differences in their performances.

Some will wobble and shake and wiggle and entice fish.

Some won't.

That's because plastic baits are made in two pieces, then sealed together and painted. They may be off a millimeter in the alignment when they are sealed. Or the paint may be a fraction of an inch thicker on one part of the lure than it is on another.

Wooden baits are not all ground exactly the same. When the notch is cut for the lips, not every notch is precisely aligned.

Some of these variations are minute, in many cases too small to notice with the naked eye. Others are big enough to easily notice. All these variations change the action of a bait.

When I get new crank baits, the first thing I do is take them out of the pack, place them side by side, and examine them.

Then I test every one to make sure the action is exactly what I want.

If I want it to throw longer and dig deeper, I add stick-on lead strips.

I test again by casting and looking for wobbles. If the bait runs to the right, I bend the line tie to the left. If it runs left, I bend the line tie to the right.

You have to tinker with your baits if you want them to perform properly.

PRESENTATION

~

Most of fishing is in the fisherman.

His choice of baits, how he presents the bait, how he works it, and what techniques he uses will decide if he catches fish.

Presenting the bait is one of the most important things to know.

There are three ways of presenting bait to a bass.

Flipping.

Pitching.

Casting.

Flipping is for close-in work, no more than 15 feet. It is the best technique to work heavy cover and a very efficient way to work without a lot of casting and reeling.

Flipping is done thusly.

Release enough line that the bait hangs down about the length of the rod. The rod is at about a 45° angle. The hand holding the rod is parallel to the water and the hand is relaxed.

With the other hand, seize the line near the reel and pull it out an arm's length. The bait is still at the length of the rod. Let the line rest gently in your open hand.

Now you are ready.

Dip the rod and swing the bait forward.

As the bait swings forward, follow in with the other hand and allow the line to slide out easily.

Don't lean forward and don't throw the bait. It's all in the wrist. Besides, you are not going for distance, you are going for accuracy and a soft presentation.

When the place you want to fish is too far away to flip, you pitch.

Pitching is for distances between 15 and 40 feet. Beyond 40 feet, you are casting.

To pitch the bait, release enough line to bring the bait back only as far as the reel. Cradle the bait in the hand that is not holding the reel. Dip the rod then swing it out sharply and release the bait. Do not throw the bait; let it be pulled gently from your hand.

A common mistake in pitching is to start with too much line. If you do this, when you release the bait it will hit the boat or the water beside the boat. Every time.

You can pitch with too little line but not with too much.

Nowhere in bass fishing is impatience more obvious than in flipping and pitching. This is because too many anglers try to jump ahead of the basics. They are going for distance when the goal is simply to put the bait where the fish is hiding and to do it as quietly as possible.

The secret in both techniques is to dip the rod in order to build the speed of the bait.

Now for casting.

There are two main ways to cast the bait: the overhead cast and the underhand cast. The underhand cast is also known as the side cast.

The overhead cast is excellent for distance. But it causes the bait to splash like a rock.

The only time you want the bait to splash is in severe conditions. If the wind is high and there are waves on the water, the fish hears the splash and comes to it out of curiosity.

The underhand cast is the best for accuracy and a quiet presentation. Stop the bait in midair, a few inches from the water, and let it fall gently.

Don't alarm the bass.

Some fishermen cast right-handed and use a left-handed retrieve reel. Others learn to cast left-handed. Many cast two-handed for distance then switch to right or left while the bait is still in the air.

It doesn't really matter how you cast. The goal is a presentation that is agreeable to the fish; a presentation that will not spook the bass.

As for accuracy, it doesn't make any difference whether you can land the bait on a quarter or a plate. But if you can put the bait on a plate as opposed to inside a Hula-Hoop, that does make a difference.

But do it gently.

Finesse it.

The single biggest problem I see with anglers is in their casting technique. Too many of them just throw it out there and plunk it into the water. They make such big splashes with their baits that you would think they are throwing stones into the water.

I was once paired with a fisherman who said getting the bait into the water without making a noise is what catches fish.

Sometimes I throw the bait up on the bank and tug it into the water so it does not splash.

A soft presentation is the ideal.

If you want to see a soft presentation—if you want to see anglers present a bait so that it just suddenly appears before a bass—watch the techniques of Rick Clunn, Jimmy Houston, and Kevin VanDam. I have fished with them and watched them.

They are consistent.

Fluid.

Precise.

Every cast results in a soft presentation.

I could watch them all day long.

Each angler has his own casting style. It's like a golf swing in that while there is an ideal, everyone does it a bit differently but with the same goal in mind.

In fishing, the goal is to get the bait from the tip of your rod to where the fish will bite it.

A good way to do that is with the roll cast.

The roll or loop cast does not build as much power as either the overhead or two-handed cast, but it does provide accuracy and quietness.

The first step in the loop cast is to release enough line so the bait dangles about a foot below the tip of the rod. Hold the rod parallel to the water. Use a small wrist motion to rotate the bait one time in a tight circle. Think of a water-skier swinging wide behind a boat and building up centrifugal force. As the bait comes out of the bottom of the loop, release it and let the speed carry it across the water.

Lower the tip of the rod, and as the bait approaches the targeted area, stop its forward motion. It falls into the water with hardly a splash; a light and delicate presentation that is good at triggering strikes.

At fishing shows or outdoor shows, you sometimes see people demonstrating this cast in a shallow pool or a tank. They can put the bait in a coffee cup from 30 or 40 feet.

Don't be intimidated by this. Many of these people are one-trick ponies who are great in a tank but couldn't do half as well in a tossing boat when the wind is blowing and the target is obscured by bushes or limbs.

If you want to watch the master of the roll cast, watch Jimmy Houston.

In calm, clear, or shallow waters, you want a very quiet presentation.

There are three ways to present the bait so delicately that it almost seems as if it has fallen off a log.

Pitching and flipping you know already.

Skip casting is the third.

The skip cast is different from all other casts. Some casts taunt the bass. Some casts make the bass curious. But the skip cast excites a bass. It makes him lose his cool and his caution.

It is a way to present the bait in places that ordinarily are difficult to reach, such as under docks and back into pockets and holes. The skip cast is used with tube baits, jigs, worms, and grubs. The spinning rod is preferred to the bait-casting rod.

First, point the rod tip toward the water. Holding it low, whip it to the rear; then fire it forward and release the bait to skip across the surface. Every time the bait hits the surface, it gets more resistance, so you have to use a lot of power.

If done properly, the skip cast causes the bass to think this is a baitfish being chased by another bass.

If you've seen minnows jumping or shad scattering while a

school of bass rounded them up like cowboys, you know what the skip cast should look like.

Bass are extremely competitive. They have to be in order to survive. If they think another bass is going for that beautiful thing fleeing across the surface, their attack mechanism is activated and they go for the bait without pausing to think. They have to beat the other bass to it.

Here's an extra technique to add to a skip cast. Once the bait has run out of power, let it slowly settle to the bottom like a wounded minnow. That way you've got two things working for you: the skitter across the surface and then the dying minnow act.

You can use the skip cast year-round; there is no season for it. It triggers the natural behavior of the bass.

SENSITIVITY

~

A bass can take your bait, roll it around in his mouth, determine it is artificial, and spit it out without your ever knowing he was there.

Sensitivity on the part of the fisherman can limit the number of those missed bass.

A good angler feels what is going on with his bait and feels when the fish mouths the bait. He knows the bait is about to hit an underwater object before it hits—and he pauses, lets the bait float up a few inches, then reels it in. He can feel the bait skip a beat or stop and knows a bass is on the line and to instantly set the hook.

A good angler is sensitive enough to know where his bait is and what it is doing even though he cannot see it.

Here are several ways to increase your sensitivity.

First, hold the rod properly. I've seen professional fishermen holding the rod behind the reel. That makes the hand and wrist work too much. It causes fatigue. It decreases sensitivity. It is not effective.

After you cast, use your hand to cradle the reel or to hold the rod just above the reel. Hold it loosely, but not loosely enough to be taken by a hard strike. I've seen bass snatch the entire rig out of the hand of an angler who was holding his rod too loosely and not paying attention.

The tighter you grasp the rod, the less sensitivity you have.

Second, let your index finger touch the line as you work the bait. The line is your direct link to the fish when you are using slow-moving baits. The rod is your direct link when you use fast-moving baits.

Third, concentrate.

If that seems basic, it is. But sometimes we become distracted by all that is going on around us, by the rhythms of nature. We must not forget why we are on the water.

The most effective techniques in bass fishing often are the simplest. If you hold your rod properly, feel the line, and concentrate on what you're doing, you will go from being an average fisherman to being an excellent fishermen.

You will know when a bass is on the line.

Most of the time.

When you are using plastic crawfish as bait, think of how the crawfish moves.

Very, very slowly.

Very small, very subtle movements.

That's because the crawfish knows if the bass sees him, his day is about to end.

The crawfish doesn't wear track shoes, so he can't run and hide. For survival, he depends on his slow movements and on his coloration.

Don't bounce a crawfish bait up and down a foot off the bottom. Make it tip-toe. Move it a half-inch at the time. This is the time for discipline. For patience.

Hold your rod very gently in your hand, so you can feel every nuance of the bottom.

Feel how easily the bait moves?

That's a rock.

Feel it pull?

You're taking it through vegetation.

Feel it grow light?

You're on a brush pile.

Feel it slide easily up something then down the other side?

That's a soft-drink can.

Feel it explode and almost jerk the rod from your hand?

That's a bass.

PATTERNS

~

Few things in fishing are discussed as much as the patterns of the bass.

Reduced to basics, finding the pattern is simply finding where the fish are located in the lake and determining what they are eating.

It goes back to food, temperature, and structure.

Finding a pattern is the foundation of bass fishing.

I was fishing a tournament on Lake Gaston in North Carolina, and the practice days were really tough. I simply couldn't figure out the pattern. I pitched and flipped docks until I turned blue. I tried a Rat-L-Trap in the backs of creeks, and I cranked secondary points and channels.

Using a Carolina rig, I caught a few fish on structure in a

creek channel. But nothing worked well enough to tell me I had found the pattern.

My first-day amateur partner said he had also caught a few on a Carolina rig. He was fishing stumps along what he thought was an old roadbed. Then we determined that what he thought was a roadbed was actually an old creek bed. We put what he had learned together with what I had learned and decided that the pattern was stumps along old creek channels. Once we found the pattern, we thumped them—caught fish like they were going out of style, and had a great day on the water.

I was the only angler in the tournament who caught a limit all three days of the competition. Not only did my partner win on the amateur side, his fish weighed more than twice as much as those caught by the amateur who placed second.

To find the pattern, I begin by eliminating as many variables as possible. Think of food, temperature, and structure. There are sub-categories within each, but these are the three main things to know.

Temperature is closely related to depth, and the depth at which the fish are holding is the first thing you need to know in developing a pattern.

One way to find the depth is to start shallow and work deeper.

The time of day should be figured into the search. After a winter night, the water is cold on the flats—those broad, open areas of relatively shallow water. That means the first deep water off the flats is warmer and will have more active fish. As the water warms during the day, fish return to the flats.

Most anglers fish shallow and look for shallow-water patterns. But shallow-water patterns can be deceptive.

One summer morning I was throwing worms against a tree line and catching lots of fish. About 10 a.m. they stopped biting. I fished up and down that bank for almost two hours and caught nothing.

Then I asked myself what the fish were doing. Where had they gone? I thought about it from the point of view of the bass. I studied the water.

Then I saw it.

As the sun rose higher, it warmed the shallow water and the fish went deeper seeking their optimum temperature.

I turned around in the boat and began fishing laydowns and stumps in deeper water. I took the same worm I had been using and tossed it out behind a stump, letting it settle to the bottom.

Thhhuuummp!

I had a fish.

I cast on another stump.

Thhhuuummp!

Another one.

The fish that had been feeding against the tree line had simply moved on to outside cover. For the rest of the afternoon, that's where I caught them.

Shallow-water patterns not only are deceptive, they can shift quickly if the weather changes. Be particularly careful of shallow water patterns after passage of a cold front.

Deep-water patterns are more difficult to find, but once you do find them, they are usually solid.

After you have determined the depth, you need to know the food and the bait that the bass are favoring. The food depends on the depth at which you find the fish and the structure or cover they are using.

They are all connected.

The fact that I catch several fish on a bait does not necessarily constitute a pattern.

Once when I was younger, I was fishing a spinner bait on a grass bank. I caught a few fish and thought I had found the pattern: spinner baits in the grass. But when I went to another grass bank, I couldn't catch any fish. Then I went back to the first grass bank and caught them again.

All I had was a spot.

If you have a similar experience, ask yourself why the fish are in that spot. Does their favoring the spot have something to do with depth or current?

The speed at which you work the bait is a crucial part of a pattern. Are you reeling fast or slow when you have a strike? You must have the presence of mind to remember on every cast what you are doing with the bait.

I was fishing Lake Sam Rayburn in Texas, reeling in a crank bait, when I turned to talk to my partner. As I turned, I gave the bait a bit of slack for half a second. A bass hit it.

On the next cast, I paused occasionally as I reeled in the bait. I caught another one.

Little things you might overlook are important to the fish. It's the little things that can help you find the pattern.

There is always more than one pattern working at any given time. Find the primary patterns and then the secondary patterns. This is not complicated. Start out with your strengths, with what you like doing the most. If you are a spinner-bait fisherman, throw spinner baits. Find the water that fits your fishing. Figure out what is available to the fish. Start eliminating variables.

The pattern I pick as my primary pattern may apply to much of the lake. But as I change positions on the lake, the conditions change and the pattern may change.

When searching for a pattern, you must focus. But you must not become too focused.

Sometimes even professional anglers analyze too much. They say a pattern might be the tips of logs or three-foot bushes on points when they should think instead of logs or point bushes.

Keep it simple.

And think like a bass.

Once you isolate the pattern and figure out what the fish are doing, you can go almost anywhere on the lake and catch a sack of fish.

It's magic when you tune in.

I was fishing Buggs Island, and during practice fishing. I identified a pattern as outside bushes and outside laydowns.

The tournament started. I ran down a bank and saw an outside laydown, and I said, "I'm going to catch a fish there." I had never fished that spot. But I caught a 5½-pounder on the first cast.

I ran down the lake and saw an outside bush, and I said, "I'll catch one there."

Another one on the first cast.

At the end of the day, I was in the lead with five fish weighing almost 25 pounds.

Once you've found a pattern, do not become locked in. Patterns can change several times in the course of a day.

The ability to quickly recognize when a pattern has changed is what separates a good fisherman from an ordinary fisherman.

If you don't find the pattern, you don't find the fish.

BURNING THE BAIT

~

On windy and overcast days, a good technique is to throw a spinner bait often and crank it hard and fast.

This is called burning the bait.

This is a clear-water technique that presents the bait to the fish quickly and causes him to make an instantaneous decision. He comes up under the bait, sees a silhouette, and doesn't have time to figure out what's going on. All he knows is that something has invaded his territory. He will hit it hard and fast.

For my spinner bait, I prefer a double-willow combination: a ¾-ounce bait with a 3½ silver willow blade in front and a 4½ gold willow in the rear. These are smaller blades than usual for this size bait, and I use them to keep the bait under the surface while it is moving fast. Some anglers believe bass prefer both blades to be gold or both to be silver. But I use one of each. I believe in covering all the bases.

Burning the bait will give you some of the best strikes you'll get as a bass angler. Tremendous strikes. The bass will try to knock the rod right out of your hand.

By the way, this technique is very taxing on the body. Burning the bait also burns your arms. You will be exhausted after several minutes. Then your second wind comes along, and you fall into a pace you can handle.

The speed of the retrieval covers almost any mistake you might make. If you've seen baitfish scattering before a school of bass, you know the baitfish are running faster than you could ever pull your bait. You can never crank as fast as Mr. Bass can swim.

So burn the bait.

MIGRATION

~

I was fishing on Lake Seminole in southwest Georgia one spring and found that the bass had come out of deep water, out of an old river channel, and were staging on a point covered with hydrilla. They were "on the grass," as we say.

But several days later, only small males were there.

The females had spawned and moved back out. But where? Where would they go?

I tried a grassy point near the spawning flats and caught 71 pounds of fish in three days.

To catch bass year-round and to catch them consistently, an angler must understand migratory patterns and staging.

Fish, like some people, have two things on their minds: eating and reproducing. For much of the year, food is their primary concern. When winter storms bring low temperatures and blustery winds, the bass moves into deep water. He's looking for the place where he can get the most food at the most comfortable temperature.

All fish have what fisheries biologists call an optimum temperature—the temperature at which things work best for them. For the bass, the optimum temperature is in the high 70s.

Unlike some trout that die when water temperatures reach the 70s, the bass is extremely hardy and can survive in water as warm as the 90s and as cold as the low 30s—a temperature spread of almost 60°F. He doesn't like such extremes, but he can survive.

So in winter, the bass goes deep because that's where the baitfish have moved, and because the water temperatures there are more stable than near the surface.

Then comes spring. And the bass begins to think of things other than food.

He feels the uncontrollable age-old need to spawn, to propagate the species. He wants to turn his lake into a bass factory. And this can be done only in warm shallow waters. If the water is too cold, the eggs will die.

The bass moves out of deep waters in late spring, bound for the spawning grounds. Bass, like birds, follow a set migratory path, an ancient route that changes little over the years. And just as birds stop and eat while they are migrating, so does the bass.

He does not rush pell-mell for the shallow flats. Instead he holds for a few days, perhaps on an outside point, any place where he can get food while he waits for the water temperatures to rise.

He is staging—hanging out, waiting. And while he is staging, he is eating heavily, fattening up before the spawn. You can catch a lot of bass on points in the early spring.

He might be here a few days or a few weeks. It depends on the temperature.

Then he moves in closer, perhaps to an inside point, and waits.

Again he is staging. He might stage three or four times before he spawns.

When bass are looking for a place to spawn, they look for areas protected from the wind. In early spring they like pockets or coves or canals, even marina basins. The bass knows that even though the waters are warming and spring is coming, a late storm from out of the North could blow in cold water. So he looks for a sun-warmed and protected area.

Coves on the north side of a lake are favorite places.

He also likes the northeast side of a lake because it catches mid-day and afternoon sun, which is warmer than the morning sun.

As the main body of the lake begins to warm and bass far removed from creeks and coves begin to spawn, the bass looks for a part of the lake with a hard bottom. Stumps and trees and bushes are favorite places to build beds.

If the lake is 60 feet deep and standing timber reaches up to or above the surface, look for bass spawning at the base of the tree limbs or in the crown of the tree.

It is all a function of temperature.

And bass like to spawn heavily on the full moon and the new moon.

After spawning, he does not rush madly back to deep water. He is thinking of food, so he hangs out where baitfish congregate. He also wants deep-water access because deep water provides security.

The bass stages both when he is moving up to the spawning grounds and when he is moving back out after spawning.

The angler is looking for the place where bass can stop during this migration, staging areas from which they can move first from deep water to shallow and then from shallow to deep.

This usually is on a point with access to deep water. And the point should have brush piles, stumps, or grass, anything that can hold baitfish. Think of cover and food.

Bass like to follow a depth contour. I have watched fish

cruising along a bank, looking for food, and they follow the depth contour. They might dart out a few feet one way or the other, chasing food, but they follow the contour.

Depth is a key ingredient in looking for bass during their migrations.

These migrations come earlier and last longer in the South. Spawning in southern states may last for six months. On the Canadian border, it might be only one month. But the basic pattern, from deep water to the shallows and back, is essentially the same.

One fall I was fishing the Thousand Islands in New York and found the fish staging as they moved toward deep water for the winter. They were holding on an old dock offshore. That was their place of safety. They would run up into the shallows to feed, then swim back out to the dock for protection.

Anglers who fish their home waters often should keep these migratory patterns in mind in the spring and fall. Just because you catch a ton of fish on one spot doesn't mean you can go back a week later and do it again.

Bass move. And the ability to understand the migration patterns and how a bass stages is what makes a good angler.

Or, as Gary Klein says, if you know where they've been and if you know where they're going, it's easy to intercept them in between.

EARLY DAYS

~

When I was young, I'd often walk down to a lake near our house to fish. The lake was about an acre and, like many Florida lakes, was dark and muddy—and filled not only with fish but with its share of snakes and alligators. I learned early to identify poisonous snakes and to pay close attention to their movements.

And I learned that they would not threaten me unless I threatened them first.

Alligators were rarely threatening, and I was not afraid of them even when wading up to my waist in the lake. Only twice did I have gators move toward me, and both times I quickly got out of the water. When you are waist-deep in dark water and an alligator is coming toward you, you don't want to hang around and wonder about his intentions.

I wore jeans and tennis shoes and waded out into the water— wade fishing—and caught gar, mudfish, catfish, and an occasional bass. As I became a better fisherman, I caught more bass and fewer of the other fish.

When I was in the eighth grade, a boy named Gerry Bevis transferred to my school. I had known him in the Boy Scouts and thought he was one of the most outstanding people I'd ever met. A few years later he was to play a big role in my decision to become a professional bass fisherman.

Gerry never allowed peer pressure to dictate what he did. He was one of those guys who, if there was any question about whether something was right or wrong, wouldn't do it. If all the guys were partying and drinking, he was the one who didn't drink. He was very focused. And no matter what he did, he did it better than anyone else.

We hit it off because he liked to fish for bass. His parents and mine used to rotate taking the two of us out to Newnans Lake on Saturday morning and leaving us there for the day. Newnans is a kidney bean-shaped lake on the eastern edge of Gainesville. It is about seven miles long, two miles wide, and surrounded by cypress trees.

During the week Gerry and I rushed home from school, did our homework, and then walked down to the lake near my house or rode our bicycles to a double lake near his house. The first lake was about six acres, and it had a little half-acre pond next to it.

Each of us carried a bait-casting outfit or a spinning outfit. We either had a small tackle box or would put a few extra baits in a baggie and leave it on the bank when we waded out into the water. Sometimes I took one of the small pocket-size tackle boxes Dad used when he went fly fishing. I dumped out all his trout supplies and put in a Hawaiian Wiggler, a Supersonic Perch, a Fleck weed-wader, a Small Oakie Bug, or plastic worms. We always had plastic worms and a few jelly worms.

One day Gerry and I went to a new pond that was filled with lily pads, other vegetation, and mud tussocks. We waded through the lily pads and walked out on the mud tussocks so we could cast our baits into clear water. I turned to walk to another spot and heard a long *whooaaaa*. I looked around and Gerry was gone. His hat was floating on the water and the tip of his rod was poking through the surface. He had stepped into a hole in the mud tussocks and disappeared.

He came to the surface and scrambled to get out of the water. He was covered with mud and yuck.

On many days, especially in the spring, Gerry and I went fishing after school, staying out until dark.

We were fearless. But that was such an innocent time. We could walk or ride our bikes anywhere. Everyone in my family fished or hunted, and they would rather see me on the water than anywhere else. My parents never worried about Gerry and me when we were fishing.

As I moved into my middle teens, my dream was to own a bass boat. Back then a boat called the Terry Bass was king of the bass boats. It was a little box-boat with stick steering for the left hand, push forward to go right and pull to go left; throttle and shifter in the right hand. Seat was up front and live well in the middle. One person could sit on a cushion atop the live well, one up forward, and one in the stern.

I used to study the classified ads, looking for bass boats, trying to hurry the day when I could afford to buy one.

Then one day there was an ad for a Perry. I thought it was a misprint and should have been Terry. I had never heard of a Perry. It was 13 feet 10 inches long, green, with a 40hp 2-cycle engine, and it cost $1,200.

Dad paid half and I paid the other half.

I didn't own a car so mom and dad pulled the boat back and forth to local lakes. Or I borrowed their car.

There were no electronics in the boat. If I wanted to know how deep the water was, I stuck my rod down until I reached mud. If I couldn't reach mud, the bottom was deeper than six feet. In that case I would drop a bait down until it hit bottom, then measure the distance on the line.

Gerry was one of the first members of the local bass club. Back then people didn't join bass clubs when they were 15 or 16. But Gerry did. And he was winning tournaments. I admired that and wondered if I could do the same.

Gerry's friendship was important to me. During those crucially formative high school years, I discovered I was not a good student. I was not good at anything. I look back today and realize I had a mild case of dyslexia and suffered from what is now known as attention deficit disorder. I was not interested in school. And there was no area where I was so good that I thought of it as a possible career. I reached out, trying everything from baseball to motorcycle racing. But no matter what I tried, there were always a ton of people better than I was.

I was becoming apprehensive about what I was going to do in my life. When I told dad, he said, "Son, you can be a ditchdigger or a doctor or whatever you want to be. But whatever you decide to do and whatever you want to be, as long as you are happy doing it, I will support you."

He did not know what a burden that vow was to become in a few short years.

Bass fishing I was good at. And I was getting better. Because of Gerry I began to think about tournament fishing.

A young angler has two types of tournaments to enter: buddy tournaments and draw tournaments.

In a buddy tournament, the two anglers choose each other. This is a team competition in which the two buddies compete against other teams. The team with the heaviest limit of bass wins anywhere from a few hundred to a few thousand dollars.

In a draw tournament, the two anglers in the boat are not a team but are fishing against each other.

The next step is the regional tournament, which can be either a buddy or a draw tournament.

If a young angler wants to become a professional, the regional tournament with a draw tournament format provides invaluable experience. This is the same format as the invitational B.A.S.S. tournaments—the professional circuit. Usually there are three days of practice before the competition. Practice days usually run Monday through Wednesday. Then the three-day tournament begins on Thursday. In the B.A.S.S. invitationals, first place wins around $42,000 in cash and prizes.

B.A.S.S. divides America into the eastern, central, and western divisions. The top fishermen in each division are invited to fish the top Pro-Am tournaments. By this time the participating anglers are considered professionals and no longer paired with other pros, but instead with amateurs. The pro in these tournaments is just that, a pro. He drives the boat and makes the decisions about where to fish.

At this level, if an angler compiles enough points to be at the top of any of the three invitational divisions, he qualifies to fish the Classic.

The winner of the Classic is considered the world-champion bass angler.

When I began fishing tournaments I was always struck by how the winners talked about their fathers.

The winner was sunburned from being out on the water. He paused as he looked into the bright glare of television cameras. Behind the lights were hundreds of other fishermen and spectators. Every year when I watched the BASS Masters Classic on television, there were more than 20,000 people attending weigh-in ceremonies on the final day.

The winner's jaw trembled. He always talked of the first time he went fishing with his dad. This was the biggest moment of his professional career. Ahead were endorsements and sponsors and a future filled with promise. But his thoughts were on the past.

He talked of how he and his dad would walk down to the creek bank or to the pond; he'd have a cane pole over his shoulder. And he remembered that special bond between him and his dad, the magic of a boy and his father fishing together. Somehow he knew, even when he was only four or five years old, that this ritual was a big step in his march toward manhood. He was doing something with his father, something that men do together.

And now he is a winner; he has proven himself a champion at something his father taught him to do.

His voice tightens and he pauses, then tears stream down his cheeks. His dad, his first fishing partner, is old now, maybe even gone on ahead. But the son remembers. He looks out in the audience for his own son, the boy he first took fishing, and senses that he is part of a long line of fishermen stretching back into the dim mists of history. He is unashamed of his tears.

Out in the audience are other fishermen who feel the same emotion he feels. And some of them remember their fathers and weep with him.

Few experiences in life have the forever magic of the first time a father and son fish together. Fathers and fishing are words that go together. They have always gone together. And they always will.

I had no sooner begun fishing local tournaments when I started wondering what it would be like to fish the tournament trail full time—to become a professional bass angler.

Until the late 1960s, when a fast-talking Alabama man named Ray Scott formed B.A.S.S., fishing contests were called derbies, and they were free-for-alls. It was a bunch of good old boys drinking and raising hell and trying to prove who could catch the biggest bass. There were no life jackets, no live wells, no kill switches on the engines, and prizes ran to ten gallons of gas and a shotgun.

There are many stories about those days, particularly about tournament-winning fish that were glassy eyed and shriveled—fish that obviously had been pulled out of the freezer for the tournament. It is said that some fish won so many tournaments, they were recognized by name.

I came along a few years later when things had settled down and bass tournaments had begun to grow a little more professional. I say "a little more professional" because, compared with the smooth professionalism of today's B.A.S.S. competitions, those tournaments were still pretty rowdy.

I remember two in particular.

My first tournament was on Lake Seminole. I was 16 and working at a grocery store and had saved enough money to pay the $50 entry fee. I went up and fished as a no-boater. The pro I was fishing with had a 135hp Mercury on the back of his boat. It was foggy, and, as we waited for the fog to burn off, he told me a bit about the lake. It was filled with stumps and standing timber. Several weeks earlier a fisherman had been running across the lake when he hit a stump. The impact flipped the engine up and over into the boat. That guy was at full speed, and all at once he had a big engine with a spinning prop in the boat with him.

It was still foggy when we took off. The sun was just coming up. We raced along, swerving around stumps and trees and flying across the water. We ran ten miles up the Chattahoochee before he shut down and was ready to go fishing.

I caught one bass.

But it was a buddy tournament I fished with Gerry that I remember most from those days.

He called and asked me to fish a tournament out of Camp Lester on the Kissimmee River. That's between Hatchineha and Kissimmee. Gerry had a 17-foot boat with an 85hp engine.

This was a big tournament. All the boats lined up across the mouth of Hatchineha. The plan was for the tournament director to race his boat in front of the long row of boats filled with contestants. If the boats were lined up properly, he was to shoot a flare and the tournament would be under way. All the contestants would simultaneously race for their fishing holes.

This was one of the infamous blastoffs, a practice so dangerous it has long since been discontinued.

Gerry and I couldn't get in the line of boats because they were wedged so closely together. Gerry's boat had an 85hp motor, while all the other boats were pushed by 125hp and 135hp engines.

We fell in behind a couple of guys and decided to follow them out of the blastoff. They were in red jumpsuits and all logoed up with patches. One of them was smoking a big cigar. Those guys were ready to go fishing.

We were two teenage boys wearing jeans and T-shirts, and we were more than a little intimidated.

The sun was just coming up, and because we were behind the bigger boats, we didn't see the tournament director running down the line. We thought there would be a little more daylight before the tournament began. Suddenly the flare exploded high in the air. As we saw it arc cross the sky, we almost panicked.

The anxious drivers of those hundred or so boats in front of us shoved their throttles forward and blasted off. Engines were screaming. It sounded like judgment day.

The guys in the red jumpsuits and the guys on both sides accelerated and blew a big hole in the water. We showered down on the throttle, shot up in the air, and all at once there was no water. We dropped four feet straight down. Rods were flying. Tackle boxes were in the air and springing open. Baits were flying. The prop was cavitating and screaming. It was absolute chaos.

We bounced our way out of there and got up to speed—if it could be called that—and I noticed the fishermen in front of us were swinging wide on the turns as they raced toward their fishing spots. I remembered tactics from my motorcycle racing days and told Gerry how to run straight lines.

We cut across the wakes of the other boats, barely cleared the point, and cut off about 20 boats on the first turn.

Then there was another turn, and again the other boats were swinging wide to enter a canal. We ran within a foot or so of the bank and passed another 40 boats.

This was the sport for me: racing boats and fishing for bass at the same time.

Our little engine couldn't compete with the big ones, but we could beat the drivers on tactics. We pulled up near the front of the pack and were in the second group of boats going through the lock.

We fished that tournament hard, caught a good sack of fish, and placed just out of the money.

Those were great days to be young and to fish tournaments. Often Gerry and I would be in his boat running four abreast down a canal with other boats, and around a corner there would be a crappie fisherman anchored in the middle of the canal. In almost every tournament, somebody ate the bank.

We all ran at full speed in thick fog. We could barely see the bow of the boat and we'd be running wide open across a lake. In one tournament, three boats were racing side by side in the fog and all were banked. No one was ever seriously hurt.

And everyone had a great time; some fishermen had a better time than others.

There was one tournament where a well known professional angler had too much to drink and stayed up all night. When he got to the lake, he passed out in his truck. Someone awakened him and he jumped in his boat and took off for the middle of the lake, where he passed out again. In the early afternoon, a competitor saw him drifting and became concerned. He approached the boat and woke his colleague. Then the hungover angler fished a few hours and won the tournament.

Someone asked him how he could drink all night, sleep most of the day, then fish a few hours and win. He said, "I came to fish."

All this changed quickly when Ray Scott and B.A.S.S. came along with the purpose of making the sport more professional. B.A.S.S. devised and implemented rigid rules that have since been copied almost word for word by almost every other tournament organization. It was Ray Scott's goal to make bass fishing a sport as professional as golf or tennis—a sport all of us could look up to and respect.

Today bass fishing is bigger than golf and tennis combined. And B.A.S.S. has become a professional, smooth running organization that sets very high standards and keeps a close eye on every phase of its tournaments. There has never been a cheating scandal in a B.A.S.S. tournament, even though in some the prize money for first place exceeds $100,000.

Bass fishing has become big business.

But sometimes I miss the old days.

HOOKS

~

If you've ever been to a seminar on bass fishing, you've heard a pro say that once you get a strike you should set the hook quickly and firmly.

"The bass has no hands," is a favorite line with the pros. They say if a bass has the bait, it has to be in his mouth and that you should jerk hard to set the hook.

Pros who use this technique don't catch every fish that strikes. I catch almost 100 percent of my strikes.

It's because I get in front of the fish.

I don't mean I position the boat a certain way relative to the fish. I mean that my hands are in the right place on the rod, that I'm thinking ahead of the fish, and that I'm in control.

It's not always good to set the hook as soon as you feel the bass. If you're checking electronics or watching an anhinga dive for fish or admiring a flock of ducks against a sunrise at the moment a bass strikes, you could be turned around with your back to the fish. Your rod could be vertical.

Set the hook immediately and you could knock your hat off, wrap the line around your head, lose your balance, and have a full-blown mess on your hands. The bass could swim a few feet, jump, and blow the bait back at you.

Here's what I recommend.

When you feel the bass, crank a couple of turns on the reel. Lower the rod toward the water. Keep your eye on the line. Make sure the bass is not tight-lining you.

All this takes about a second and a half.

You know the bass is there, but he must not know you are there. Don't let him feel you. He will blow the hook.

Now you are ahead of the fish.

Set the hook.

Now he knows you are there.

But you are in control.

This technique is for worms and jigs, baits you have to set the hook on. Active baits such as crank baits and spinner baits give you no choice about when to set the hook. The bass hits them hard. When that happens, you have to jerk hard in response.

But with plastic worms, jigs, crawfish, Texas or Carolina rigs, you have a choice. It takes a moment for the bass to figure out what is going on.

If you feel him before he feels you, you have him.

You are in control and you can bring him to the boat.

There are so many books, magazine and newspaper articles, and TV shows out there about how to catch a bass. If an angler listens and reads enough and begins to consistently catch fish, he thinks he has discovered the secret of the universe. And that his way is the only way to do it.

Hook setting is a good example.

Many anglers think a side set, in which they do a half-pivot away from the fish and keep the rod almost parallel to the water, is the only way to set a hook. It's something of a bank-and-yank maneuver, and if the angler is not careful, he can lose his balance; or if he pivots too far, lose sight of the fish.

The idea behind the hook set is simple: get the line tight and apply quick pressure.

There is more than one way to do this.

The bass doesn't know if you are using a side set or an overhead set; all he knows is that he is being caught.

I prefer something between the side set and the overhead set.

Call it an offset hook set.

When you rear back, pull the rod toward your shoulder. It doesn't matter which shoulder, right or left. What is important is that there is more power with this hook set because your arms are close to your body. It is efficient.

There is room for variation. But the object is to be efficient.

Just don't do an overhead set in line with your body. If the bait flies out of the water, you could have two sets of treble hooks rocketing for your face.

THE NEXT CAST

~

When I was 15 or 16 and really getting into fishing, I'd be riding in a car with mom and dad, looking out the window for lakes. Every time I saw a lake, my first thought would be, *Where are the fish hiding?*

As we drove past, I'd looked at the grass points, pockets, trees, clumps of lily pads—the good ambush spots where a bass might lurk.

There should be a bass on that point.

I bet one is hiding up there in the grass.

I analyzed every lake.

A common mistake I see among bass fishermen is that they don't know where to make the next cast.

If there is a grass line, they will throw on it somewhere. If there is a tree, they will throw on it.

But they don't know where to throw for the highest probability of catching a fish. They simply throw and hope.

I'm always looking one or two casts ahead, figuring out where the bass will be and analyzing the available targets.

If I'm with another tournament angler, a professional, I know that if I don't make the cast, he will.

This is a big difference between a beginning angler and a professional angler. The beginning angler doesn't realize where fish are supposed to be located. The professional does.

Or he should.

The idea is not simply to get out on the water and pursue the fish. The idea is to catch them.

One of the great experiences of my professional career was to be the commentator for the television show of the BASS Masters Classic. I was in a camera boat following the best bass fishermen in the world. I would see where an angler was going, and I would turn to the cameraman and whisper, "He's about to catch a fish on that bush coming up."

But the contestant wouldn't always make the cast.

That's why some anglers catch fish one day and not the next. They catch the easy ones. But when the fish are in tight cover or target oriented, haphazard casts won't catch them.

I never make a random cast.

I make every cast thinking I am going to get bit.

SHADE

~

Orange Lake is about 20 minutes southeast of Gainesville and is considered one of the best bass lakes in Florida. I was fishing there with Gerry Bevis.

He was up front casting about 45° off the bow, and I was in the stern casting forward at about 45°. The sun was abeam.

Gerry was catching one fish after another. He was thumping them.

I was catching nothing.

Then I realized what was happening. Gerry was fishing in the sunlight out beyond the boat, and I was casting in his shadow.

The bass saw the shadow and thought it signified a bird or some other predator. The bass would not bite.

The bass is wary.

Never fish in the shadow of your partner or in your own shadow.

C.A.B.O.

~

My sister married the manager of a camera store in Gainesville. He and I fished tournaments together for a while. I called him "Mr. Cheeseburger," because on the way to a tournament, he always ate a cheeseburger for breakfast. Three-thirty or four o'clock in the morning and he ate cheeseburgers.

He wanted me to meet a girl who worked at the camera store. Her name was Polly Fivecoat. I kept putting it off. But one day he called and said, "Here she is," and then he put her on the phone.

She was embarrassed and I was embarrassed. But I invited her to dinner at a Chinese restaurant and found that she liked to fish, that she could repair cars, and that she loved the outdoors.

Before I could invite her out again, I caught a severe case of poison ivy and couldn't get out of the house for several weeks. She called to see how I was. We talked for a long time. We talked about everything under the sun.

When I was well, I took her fishing on the Suwanee River. Later we went swimming in the cold, clear springs near the river. Then she showed up at weigh-in during a tournament I had entered.

Eighteen months later I took her back to the Chinese restaurant where we had our first date and proposed.

It was Easter. I gave her an Easter basket. Inside the basket was an engagement ring.

We were married August 23, 1980.

The wedding ring she gave me had the initials C.A.B.O. on the inside.

"What does that mean?" I asked.

"Think about it."

I told her I couldn't figure it out.

"Catch a big one."

Beyond the sentiment, I sensed another message. Polly was making a promise to support my fishing. She knew that fishing makes me happy.

As I began to fish more and more tournaments, Polly took over all the scheduling and countless details of travel. She knew that my job was to fish; and that if I had to worry about all the business details, my mind was not on fishing.

I caught a good one.

HONOR

~

I was 23, another Joe Fisherman, when I saw a flyer in a Gainesville tackle store about a tournament at Lake Talquin on the Ochlockonee River. I entered and drove up to fish as a no-boater.

I drew as a partner a fisherman who was a guide on the lake. In the first hour of the tournament, he caught a couple of fish, then maneuvered the boat so he got the first cast at every stump and log before I could reach it. He would cast a few times and move on, and I had to fish behind him. He was not giving me an equal chance with the fish.

And...he was fishing too fast.

I threw a plastic worm where he had just fished and peeled the line off my reel as he moved to a nearby stump.

I caught a three-pounder.

He moved to another log. I threw in behind him, let the worm sink to the bottom, then worked the bait.

I caught a two-pounder.

He caught two fish that day.

I caught eight.

He became so angry that he went to weigh-in when there was still more than an hour of fishing time left.

My eight fish came in at more than 18 pounds. I won the tournament by an ounce and received a check for $1,000. Up to that time it was my biggest check. And it seemed like a fortune. I realized that maybe I was good enough to fish the trail as a professional. Maybe, just maybe, I could become one of those fortunate people who lives his dream.

On stage, I thanked my partner for putting me on the fish. I said that he found the fish, that he knew they were on the stumps and logs, that I was new to the lake and didn't know where they were. I said I was still young as a tournament fisherman and would never have found the fish without him.

I realized then, and I have seen it many times on the water, that no matter how hard you try to take advantage of someone, they will get their licks in. What goes around comes around. The best way to do business is to be straightforward and let it happen how it will.

There must be honor on the water.

And in life.

I BREAK THE LINE

~

I went to the University of Florida for four years and never got a degree. Many weekends when I should have been studying, I was fishing. And each year when spring came, I had to be on the water. Time after time I dropped out of school to go fishing.

This drove dad nuts. He had a Ph.D., had been chairman of the sociology department, and his son couldn't get past the sophomore level.

My sister had graduated summa cum laude and gone on to get a master's degree. I was dropping out of school to go fishing.

Dad took an early retirement to run a pest-control business he had invested in several years earlier. He needed help, so I dropped out of the university for good and went to work for him. We had not gotten along well for a year or so. He was very demanding and wanted me to do everything his way.

I thought we were close enough that I could work for him and still have time to go fishing.

I was wrong.

The pest-control business supplied horse and poultry farms across the country. Our product was a natural one—that is, we raised wasps to control the flies. The wasps are parasites of the housefly; to keep the wasps alive, we raised millions of fly larvae, or maggots. Maggots require attention 7 days a week and 365 days a year. There was little time off for me.

I found working for my dad almost impossible. I know now that it is natural for a son to want to do things his way and for a father to want everything done his way. A natural tension exists between father and son as the son enters manhood and begins designing his own life.

It was becoming more and more difficult for me to live up to dad's expectations. I saw him as an amazing man. He had wired our house. He did the plumbing. He made the cabinets. He fixed things around the house and did all the mechanical work on his car. He taught me how to do many of those things.

He hoped I would give up fishing and run what had become the family business. He began to criticize the time I spent fishing.

I had fished a lot of local, state, and regional tournaments and was learning to fish in other lakes in other states. I was learning how to fish reservoirs and rivers. My skills as an angler were continuing to grow.

I was saving money. I wanted enough to support Polly and me for two years while I fished the tournament trail. Two years would be long enough for me to find out if I had what it took to become a professional bass angler.

I brought in another employee who was willing to work days

on end so I could fish tournaments. He nicknamed dad "Pops."

Hiring someone to work in the family business so I could go fishing did not seem like a good business decision to dad. He thought fishing was for fun and that business was how a person made his livelihood.

Time after time when the subject came up, dad would take a big puff off his cigarette, blow smoke in the air, and say, "Son, if you spent as much time at business as you do at fishing, you would make a million dollars. You can't make any money fishing. You can't support Polly that way."

We grew farther and farther apart.

Dad didn't understand one thing: Fishing was the only thing I really loved. Even though bass fishing was just beginning to be recognized as a profession, it was the first thing and the only thing I had found in my life that gave me focus and direction. When I was fishing, I was gold. Fishing said to me, "You have value."

I was winning tournaments. No longer was I just another guy back in the pack. Fishing had become more than just something to do. It was my life.

I know that fishing is not up there with finding a cure for cancer. It is not a life-saving endeavor. But neither is knocking a ball around a golf course. Or driving a race car in a circle. Or bouncing a basketball up and down the court.

Nevertheless, for me, fishing was a noble profession.

The first disciples were fishermen. And Peter, the rock upon whom the early church was founded, was known as "The Big Fisherman."

But my dad wanted me to raise maggots.

One day I was installing PVC pipe at the plant. I had done it a thousand times when dad was not there. But this time he was there and he began telling me how to do it.

"Dad, I've done this before. I know what I'm doing."

He was furious at me for not listening, and I was furious at him for not letting me be me.

We started yelling at each other.

I grabbed him and looked him in the eye, and almost decked him.

But I controlled it. I threw down my tools and walked off.

From then on, my dad and I were not friends. I didn't even consider him a father. He was someone I had to deal with at work. He was my adversary. We had to work together. Polly and I would join him, mom, and my sister's family for holidays. But we had no relationship.

Grown men, married men who are thinking of raising a family, do not become professional bass fishermen—not in the world of a former university professor. Dad thought I was a failure.

Four or five years later, he turned the business over to me and retired. I think he hoped that, once the business was mine, I would give up the idea of fishing and would settle down, expand the business, and make some serious money.

That was 1984: the year I made the decision to become a professional bass fisherman.

RHYTHMS

~

The bass fisherman must have a sense of what is going on around him, not just on the water but all around him.

I was on a lake and noticed the cows on a distant hillside were sleeping. Not a bird was in the air. No baitfish were jumping. Bugs and mosquitoes were inactive. Bass were not biting. All was quiet.

Then suddenly the cows stood up and began grazing. Birds were flying about and landing and feeding. Baitfish were darting about in schools. Mosquitoes were buzzing around my head.

And bass began biting anything I threw at them.

I don't pretend to understand this. But I do know the sun and the moon have strong effects on all creatures. And I do believe a bass fisherman must become part of the rhythms of nature. It is more than the passive observation of what is going on around us. It is the understanding that all wild creatures are tied together by invisible links. A hawk flying overhead, a heron wading in the shallows, a deer gazing from the thick bushes along a riverbank— all can tell you about the bass…if you listen.

As fishermen, we can take advantage of nature's mood swings. Things happen. A switch is turned on somewhere and creatures become excited; they are on the move, they begin to feed.

We bass fishermen are not simply observers passing through the natural world. We are part of that world.

The more we understand this, the more fish we will catch.

TIP

~

Many pros don't like to use a trailer hook because it can easily be snagged in bushes or grass. They say they never use a trailer hook until they miss a few bass.

When I hear that, I want to tell them I am catching the fish they are missing. And I am catching them on a trailer hook.

Why wait until you miss several fish before utilizing a piece of equipment that would have caught them in the first place? You might not get another chance at those fish. One of the fish you missed could have won a tournament for you.

I always use a trailer hook on spinner baits and buzz baits.

If it snags frequently, I'll take it off. But I always begin by using a trailer hook.

Always.

I can't count the number of times I have been slow-rolling a spinner bait in the grass and felt a bass come up and nip at the backside of the bait. When he does, it is the trailer hook that gets him.

In almost every tournament I fish, from a quarter to one-half of the fish I catch are caught on a trailer hook.

These are fish I might not have felt but certainly would have missed without the trailer hook.

Why wait until you miss them?

GET HIM ON

~

Too many fishermen are afraid to put the bait where the fish is.

They don't want to put the bait in lily pads, matted cover, thick weeds, or tangled laydowns because they think they might snag the bait, or, if they hook a fish, they might not be able to pull it out.

But bass love heavy cover. They like hiding up under lily pads. They like thick weeds. And tangled laydowns are one of their favorite places.

So put the bait there.

Don't worry about getting hung up or getting him out.

Worry about getting him on.

THE BASS

~

Some days the bass is tricky.

Some days he is cautious.

Some days he is ferocious.

Every day he is magic.

When I first began fishing tournaments, there were days when I caught nothing. I began saying to myself, "Today I am not going to get skunked," and I began to consistently catch one or two fish.

Then I began catching limits.

"Oh, man. I caught a limit today," I would say to anyone who would listen.

Then I learned more about the bass and his habits and why he was there; what bait he might want and where to throw the bait; how to throw it and how to work the bait. Then I began catching keepers—fish bigger than the tournament's minimum acceptable size. I began catching a limit of keepers.

Catching a limit of keepers is a special plateau.

Then consistently catching a limit of keepers became the goal.

"I'm going to use a bigger bait and work it slower," I told myself. I figured out that I was getting big bites on buzz baits or big bites flipping in heavy cover. I began to sense levels of progression as an angler.

The angler should constantly see progression in his competition with the bass. But no matter how good he gets, the angler will never be as good as he would like.

There is always more to learn.

The greatest thing about bass fishing is to take the times you don't catch many fish and turn those times into learning experiences. Figure out what you did wrong. Talk to the guys who did catch them. Read interviews with other anglers and remember what they did that worked out on the water. Talk to the winners and ask, "How did you do it?" They will talk to you.

No matter how much you learn and no matter how good you get, there will be days when the bass wins. That is why the bass is the greatest fish in the world. You will never figure him out 100 percent.

Take Rick Clunn. He is consistently the best bass fisherman who ever walked. He was the first to make more than a million dollars fishing the tournaments. He is a tremendous angler. And he says you have to learn to lose as well as you've learned to win. He has bad days. Roland Martin and Larry Nixon have bad days. But those days can be learning experiences.

You can learn as much when you don't catch fish as when you do.

You may even learn more.

COLOR

~

Some fishermen think color is the great secret of this sport. One of the biggest, longest running and most controversial debates in bass fishing involves color.

Are fish color-blind?

Can bass recognize different colors?

If so, what color will get the most bites?

I've talked to fisheries biologists about this and been told there is no supporting evidence for studies indicating fish can determine colors. Dr. Bob Reinert, a fisheries professor at the University of Georgia, says colors do allow a fish to detect contrast. He says that fishermen and not fish are concerned with colors—a fact the tackle industry appreciates.

Anglers buy purple and pink worms that don't match anything in the environment. They like these colors and assume the bass will also like them.

Even if bass could determine colors, so what? Nothing shows that color determines whether or not a bass will hit the bait.

All the hoopla about color is just that—hoopla.

I use dark baits in dark water and lighter baits in clear water. Beyond that, I don't think color is the most important factor in having a good day on the water.

The size of the bait is more important than the color. The depth of the bait and the speed of the bait are more important than the color.

You could be fishing a nine-inch worm and getting no bites. But switch to a seven-inch and they will take it.

Where and how you present the bait is far more important than color. If the fish is there and I put the bait in front of him, I'll get the bite.

Remember what is important to a bass.

Size of the bait.

Speed of the bait.

Depth of the bait.

Presentation.

Then color.

Maybe.

I BECOME A PROFESSIONAL ANGLER

~

In the spring of 1984, I went on the tournament trail as a full-time professional bass angler.

My first year was a great year.

I was Florida's Angler of the Year on the Red Man Tournament Trail and, for the first time, qualified for a $100,000 tournament. It was held on Lake Tohopekaliga near Orlando, about an hour south of Gainesville.

I had a two-day practice, an off-day to make final preparations for the biggest tournament of my life, and then a two-day competition.

On the off day, Polly told me she was pregnant with our first child.

On one hand I was thrilled. We wanted to have children. But I was just getting started on the tournament circuit. My ability to support my family depended on how many fish I caught. Bass were not going to jump into the boat to help me out financially. I had visions of having to go back to the pest control business in order to make ends meet.

"Boy, I better win this tournament," I said.

The first day of the tournament I weighed in and had a two-pound lead. In most lakes, this would be a comfortable lead. But we have such big bass in Florida, a two-pounder is nothing. I was far from comfortable.

I've never fished harder than I did the second day of that tournament. At weigh-in I had a four-pound lead.

I won the tournament and a check for $100,000.

My dad was in the crowd when it was announced that I had won. He had always been worried that I could never make money as a professional bass angler.

He was so proud, maybe prouder than I was.

I think that was the day when he realized that fishing was a lot more than fun—that fishing could be a good career choice.

That big win so early in my career made it easier for him when, two years later, I said, "Pops, I want to sell the business."

But he was disappointed, too. We had worked hard to build up the business and make it realize its potential. But the $100,000 check showed him that bass fishing had as much potential as raising maggots.

"Shaw is a respected veteran of the tournament trail and top-notch fisherman. But he is respected also for his character and his integrity. He takes a long-range view of this sport and is the epitome of what I would want this sport to be. He is the perfect spokesman for all professional bass fisherman. He has class and integrity, is a great fisherman, and an excellent speaker— the total package of professionalism. And his celebrity has not gone to his head. He is the same guy he was ten years ago."

—Jay Yelas

HP

~

One day the phone rang and on the other end was a man named Tommy Clark.

"You the fisherman?" he asked.

He said he had invented a hook that would increase my catch. He couldn't have called at a better time. I was hooking fish, but I was losing a lot of them. I told him I would love to see his hook.

We met at an Italian restaurant. I signed a non-disclosure form, and he showed me the hook. It was an innovative design with a wide gap and a deep pocket. But it needed some modifications, and I needed to prove it on the water.

We changed the clip that holds the bait on, changed the angle of the shaft and the length of the shaft, and a few other things, then I began fishing the hook.

Tommy would hand-bend two or three hooks for each tournament. I gave a couple of the hooks to Larry Lazoen, a fellow angler and good friend. We only had two each. They were so effective—and so rare—that if we snagged one, we were ready to go swimming to retrieve it.

Larry and Randy Behringer, another angler, were rooming together during a tournament in Texas. Randy saw one of the hooks on Larry's bed, picked it up and said, "Is this the hook that Shaw has been talking about so much?"

He said he had been flipping a craw and losing a bunch of fish. He wanted to try the new hook. The next day he caught a 19-pound stringer and jumped into the money. "Man, that is one awesome hook," he said.

The hook drastically improved the number of fish I caught. Rarely would I get a strike and not hook him. And when I hooked him, he stayed hooked.

After I placed third in a tournament on Lake Mead, we decided the hook was ready to go to market. We called it the High Performance or HP hook.

Many nights Tommy and I and our wives were up until early in the morning packaging and mailing hooks.

By 1990 the hook was commercially available and winning almost every tournament in which it was used. Many hook manufacturers began making similar hooks. In 1995, Eagle Claw bought the hook and marketed it as the Shaw Grigsby HP hook.

Today it remains the best hook available for soft plastics and Carolina rigs.

KEEP FISHING

~

A year after I won the $100,000 tournament, I was fishing a regional tournament on Lake Sinclair. The editor of a bass fishing magazine was in the boat with me. She was there to write a story about how I was defending my title.

Fishing with a woman in a small open bass boat is handled in a very straightforward manner. Before we left the marina, I reminded her that the boat had no toilet facilities, that I would have to relieve myself from time to time, and that she should make her plans accordingly.

It was late morning when I told her I had to pee and could she please turn her head. I continued to cast.

A bass hit the bait.

"There's one," I said as I set the hook.

She turned around and began taking pictures.

I couldn't stop and zip up my pants with a fish on the line. I was fighting to defend my title. So I reeled fast and boat-flipped the bass over my shoulder. It was a three-pounder.

Then I finished, made myself presentable, turned and put the fish in the live well.

When a professional angler is in his boat, he never stops fishing.

Inevitably it is the cast that you don't make that counts. Once a partner and I pulled up on a good spot, and I said, "Throw it there."

He said, "I have to go."

I threw it on the spot and caught a big one.

I can't tell you how many times a partner has stopped fishing in that situation, and I caught a big one that he might have caught.

Missing a single cast can cause an angler to miss the fish that would have won the tournament.

We fish all the time.

Even when nature calls.

REALITY

~

When I first became a pro, I set three goals. I wanted to win a boat and a motor. I wanted to win a B.A.S.S. tournament. And I wanted to fish the BASS Masters Classic.

I won a boat and motor in 1985. But my other two goals were much more difficult. That might surprise amateur anglers who think that professionals win and win and win.

I used to think that way.

But after a slow first year on the B.A.S.S. tournament trail, I got a copy of the BASS Masters Classic Report and looked at the stats on the performances of the best fishermen in the world to see how they had placed in various tournaments.

It was an inspiration.

It turned my thinking around.

Every angler should study the Classic Report.

Some of the very top guys, the legends, the guys whose names are known to every bass fisherman in the country, had placed 95th in one tournament or 190th in another. Those guys had many tournaments when they didn't make a check.

I sat down and analyzed the numbers.

It was astonishing then, and it's still astonishing.

The top bass fishermen in the world, the best of the best, win only about 5 percent of the B.A.S.S. tournaments they enter. That's five wins out of a hundred tournaments entered.

Rick Clunn, a world-class fisherman who has qualified for the Classic 25 times, has entered 234 tournaments in his career.

He finished first in12.

That's 5 percent.

Larry Nixon has entered 203 tournaments and won 13 —that's 6 percent.

Denny Brauer has entered 176 tournaments and won 10 —or 5 percent.

Gary Klein has entered 180 tournaments and won 7 —3 percent.

And Roland Martin, one of the old-timers in this business, has entered 209 tournaments and placed first 9 percent of the time.

After studying the Classic reports and seeing how other anglers performed, I realized that I could compete at that level.

I realized that an angler does not have to win all the time to qualify for the Classic. No one wins all the time. An angler makes the Classic by placing consistently in B.A.S.S. tournaments.

Understanding the reality of competitive fishing gave me the strength to get up and get back on the trail. The new understanding changed my mental attitude and gave me the confidence to say, "I can compete with those guys."

I qualified for the Classic in 1986, my second full year on the tournament trail.

BALANCE

~

After I won the $100,000 tournament and qualified for the Classic, I suddenly had a reputation. Other bass fishermen wanted to hear what I had to say. I began doing fishing seminars all over the country and making promotional appearances at sports shows. Sponsers became more interested. I was being pushed and pulled in half a dozen directions. I was new at this and did not know how to manage my time. Plus I enjoyed the recognition that came with being considered a top fisherman. I had never been a top anything.

I was so busy with the business of being a new celebrity that I did not qualify for the Classic in 1987.

It occurred to me that I was about to become a flash in the pan. I couldn't spend all my time at seminars or being a celebrity—not if I wanted to become one of the top bass anglers in America.

So I sat down and seriously thought about what had happened and how I could change it. It was difficult for me to admit the obvious: I needed to spend more time on the water and less time being a celebrity.

I needed to learn the secret of balance.

I began fishing hard, and soon I was making a check in almost every tournament I entered.

I qualified for the 1988 Classic.

It's all a question of balance.

A new professional angler must decide what his priorities are and what is important to his career.

With me, it's fishing.

It has always been fishing.

But for awhile, I almost forgot.

EQUIPMENT

~

When I am on the water, I often see lures left high in trees or in bushes as a result of an errant cast. The angler cut his line and the bait remained.

When the water is clear, I sometimes see lures snagged on structure eight or ten feet below the surface.

On those occasions I pull out my plug pole. Not many fishermen carry these. A plug pole is a telescoping aluminum pole with a corkscrew of heavy-gauge wire at the end. It extends to about 20 feet, far enough to reach the limbs of many trees. And it will go deep enough to reach a plug that I, or another angler, might have snagged.

A plug pole cost about $80.

I see and retrieve a lot of plugs.

I retrieved enough plugs in six months to pay for the plug pole.

MY FIRST B.A.S.S. WIN

~

There are several tournament organizations out there today. But B.A.S.S. remains far and away the most prestigious. Win a single B.A.S.S. tournament and people know your name. Win two and you are a star. Win three and you're pushing the superstar category.

I won a number of other tournaments before I managed to win a B.A.S.S. tournament—achieving the third goal I had set when I became a pro.

My first B.A.S.S. win was in March 1988, on Lake Sam Rayburn in Texas.

During my pre-fishing days, I found the mother lode of bass. I was catching 8- and 9-pounders, and even saw a 13-pounder. I was stunned. I thought I could break the weight record for seven fish and do it with only five fish.

I thought that when the tournament started, I would catch a 40-pound stringer. I had visions in my head of what it would do to my young career to win a prestigious B.A.S.S. tournament.

The next three days could be the most important of my professional life.

The first day of competition I told my partner, who happened to be fishing his first tournament, "I'm on them. We are going to catch them today."

And we did. I caught five bass weighing 28 pounds, 11 ounces. Twenty pounds is a good stringer in tournament fishing. I was in the lead and knew I could win the tournament.

The second day I caught a 12-pound stringer and was in the lead by 4 pounds.

One more day to glory.

The third day, the last day of the tournament, I awakened and didn't have to look out the window to know the weather was lousy. It was bitterly cold, and the wind was blowing from the North at more than 25 miles an hour. Five-foot waves were rolling through the protected waters of the marina. A bass boat couldn't have survived out on the open waters of the lake.

Rayburn had turned vicious.

Until then it was a given that a tournament continued no matter how bad the weather. And it was a given that a B.A.S.S. tournament lasted three days.

For the first time in history, B.A.S.S. called a tournament because of weather. After only two days, this tournament was over.

I was in shock.

Someone stuck a camera in my face and said, "How do you

feel about winning this tournament, about your first B.A.S.S. win?"

I said I didn't feel too good about it.

I didn't want to face the other contestants, not after winning this way. I wanted to win the way fishermen had always won. I wanted to prove I could catch fish under those extreme conditions. I wanted to prove I would have caught enough fish to win if the tournament had gone the third day.

I grabbed my partner and said, "We're going fishing."

He looked at the four- and five-foot waves, listened to the howling wind, and shivered in the bitter cold. But he was game.

We cut across the cove to one of my backup spots. On the second bush I cast on, I caught a 2½-pounder. And I knew I could have caught the limit that day. So I came in and accepted the win.

Today if conditions on the water are such that the lives of fisherman may be endangered, the tournament is called. It doesn't happen often. But it happens enough to affect the strategy of anglers.

For instance, if an angler is leading a tournament on the second day and he knows severe weather is coming in, he goes to his best hole and catches every big fish he can.

That time at Rayburn was the only time I've ever won a B.A.S.S. tournament in two days. Since then, there have been a few times when I was leading on the second day and saw a cloud on the horizon, and I asked the tournament director to call the tournament early.

DAD

~

It was fishing that separated my dad and me, and it was fishing that brought us back together.

He slowly began to accept the fact that I was not going to

follow his idea of what my life's work should be, and that maybe fishing could be more than a sport.

The tension between us began to ease.

Even though he had retired and was in his 70s, he was still an active man. One day when I was about to fish a tournament down on Lake Okeechobee in southern Florida, I went to him and, on the spur of the moment, said, "Pops, do you want to go with me?"

He looked at me in surprise. Then delight. "Yes, son."

I told him he couldn't smoke in the car or the hotel room. So every time we stopped for gas, he jumped out and puffed and puffed, then smudged the butt. He hated to throw a cigarette away.

Dad fished the back of the boat during practice days. He made a spinner-bait skirt out of little flashy tinsel. He always wanted to throw something wild to catch bass. He enjoyed tinkering with sparkly baits that looked like Christmas trees. He put that spinner bait on and went fishing.

We hadn't been on the water long when I heard him grunt. Dad always grunted when he caught a fish.

It was a big chain pickerel, the southern version of the northern pike.

He caught a second one.

"Yeah, Pops, you got that pickerel bait going," I said.

He never caught a bass on that spinner bait. But the pickerel loved it.

We had a great day on the water.

After that, dad began going with me to tournaments, and we fished together during the practice days.

He was always tinkering. He became interested in scents and began dipping his baits into bottles and cans of oils and all sorts of stinky stuff that he had mixed together. I still have jackets with his fish scent on them. It will never come out.

Then he wanted to make baits that emitted sounds. He put

together some of the strangest contraptions I have ever seen. He began experimenting with hydrophones and using batteries from a hearing aid to power electronic noisemakers. He even tried hanging rattles on spinner baits.

"Dad, stick with the basics. Stick with the basics," I kept saying.

But dad was always out there looking for the home run.

Things were still a bit strained between us. But when I look back, I realize that as the tension between us eased, we came together—as father and son, as friends.

We were fishing partners again.

TIP
~

Bass often lurk in the shadows.

Logs, blowdowns, docks, old barges, and stumps—anything in the water is good cover for the bass and should be fished.

It is better to throw a bait parallel to a log than across it.

Fish blowdowns by casting from the crown of the tree toward the roots. That way, as you retrieve the bait, it is less likely to snag the limbs.

Fish both sides of a blowdown.

Fish the shady side of stumps.

Conventional wisdom says bass like the shade because they have no eyelids and the sunshine hurts their eyes. Or because the slightly lower temperatures are closer to their comfort zone.

But I think they like the shade because the lower light levels offer camouflage and aids in ambushing passing fish.

Think like the bass.

It is easier to ambush fish from the shady side than it is from the sunny side.

Remember, the bass is a predator.

THE PRO

~

There are three ways to make a living as a professional bass angler.

First, you can be a phenomenal angler and win a lot of tournaments.

Second, you can be a very good promoter of fishing-related products. If you are a great salesman and can promote a sponsor's products well enough to make an impact on his bottom line, you don't have to be a good fisherman. In fact, you can be a mediocre fisherman if you are a great promoter.

Third, you can combine these two, which is what many anglers do. We are good fishermen and good salesmen.

Today if you want sponsors you have to be relatively young, relatively handsome, relatively articulate, and very quick on your feet. You have to look good and sound good. You have to like being in front of a crowd.

Most of all, you have to be able to move product.

The biggest misconception I see today among professional anglers is that they think if they are good fishermen, they should be paid for every product they use. "Show me the money," they say to potential sponsors. They don't understand that being a good fisherman is not enough. There are plenty of good fishermen who can't move product.

When I approached my first sponsor, I worked the first year free. "Let me show you what I can do for you," I said. "Let me work for you for a year and then we will talk money."

It worked fine. The more I produced for him, the more he produced for me.

The only reason an angler should be paid by a sponsor is if he is making money for the sponsor.

Catching fish is only part of being a professional fisherman. And catching fish is not enough.

Not today.

PLANES, MAPS, AND GPS

~

Any body of water that an angler has not fished before must be approached scientifically.

It is expensive, but professional anglers generally agree on the methodology.

First we study topo maps to familiarize ourselves with the new water. We look for cover and structure. We look for depths.

Then we come to the water before the tournament, charter an airplane and fly over the lake. If it is a river, we fly a hundred miles upstream and downstream. A hundred miles is less than a two-hour run in a bass boat.

We look for creek channels, deep-water areas, shallow flats, grass beds and heavy cover. We consider the water temperature, water clarity, the wind, shade, and bottom composition.

Then, with seasonal migrations in mind, we try to get an overall feeling for what the pattern might be.

As we look out of the airplane and see the most likely bass habitats, we mark the locations on a hand-held Global Positioning System (GPS). Once we are on the water we can run straight to those locations.

When you are fishing for $100,000, it is good to know where you are going before you get there.

FAITH

~

By 1989 I considered myself a proficient bass fisherman, one who had realized major accomplishments in the sport. But something was missing. That's hard to explain, because I had the best wife in the world, great kids, and was pursuing my dream of making a living as a professional angler.

I had everything but it was not enough.

Then Terry Chupp gave me a tape.

Let me explain. When anglers check into a B.A.S.S. tournament, there is a long line of people who represent equipment manufacturers. They give us bags of stuff, hoping we are using their lure or their fishing line when we win the tournament. They know that if we like the products, we will talk them up. And when pros start talking about equipment, other anglers will buy that equipment.

Terry Chupp had a booth at the sign-ins and gave out bibles. *Who cares?* I thought. I took a lot of bibles from Terry and stuck them in the corner. Then he gave me a tape and said it was Hank Parker's testimony.

I didn't know what a testimony was, but I did know that Hank Parker was one of the premier anglers in this sport. I put the tape in my suitcase.

In November I was coming back from a tournament in Lake Havasu, out in Arizona. Dad was sleeping. I don't know why, but I pulled the Hank Parker tape from my suitcase and put it in the tape deck.

As I listened to the tape, I suddenly realized why I was not happy. I suddenly realized that even though I thought I had everything, I did not have the one thing that was most important.

I did not have God in my life.

On January 22, 1990, I was fishing a tournament on Lake

Okeechobee and went out to dinner with Terry Chupp. We went to a Chinese restaurant. Terry preached the gospel to me that night. And then over a bowl of hot-and-sour soup, he and I prayed.

I placed third in that tournament, began catching lots of fish, and realized that I was now complete. I was truly happy.

And I began seeing signs that I was being protected.

I had fished a tournament in Texas and was passing through Shreveport when I pulled into a service station for gas. Another bass fisherman, Steve Daniels, was behind me. He followed me into the service station, got out of his car and said, "You need to check your tire. I saw sparks flying from it."

The bearings on the trailer had burned out. I interrupted my trip and went to a nearby motel while the bearings were replaced. I was on the way back to the service station when the transmission in my truck failed.

I was near a boat dealer who knew me. I had done a favor for him earlier and forgotten about it. But he hadn't. And he took care of me.

If my competitor had not stopped me when he did, I would not have noticed the problem with the bearings until I was past Shreveport and into that lonesome stretch of highway going toward Monroe. There is nothing along that stretch of road. And most likely that is where my transmission would have failed.

Repairing the bearings and the truck would have been very difficult out there. It would have taken awhile.

But it happened in downtown Shreveport.

You might say, "You were lucky that this happened where it did." But it wasn't luck. It was time for the bearings to burn out and the transmission to fail, and it could have happened in a really bad place. But it happened where the repair work was easy.

A lot of things happen to us that we call luck or coincidence when it is neither.

On the first night of a fishing tournament, the Christian Anglers always meet. Out of around 300 fishermen, we might have as many as 90 show up for meetings. I'd say a third or more of the professional anglers are serious Christians.

My life changed when I became a Christian. With my new faith, I realized that with Jesus I was strong enough to handle whatever came into my life.

I did not know then how soon and how seriously my faith would be tested.

FISHING WITH DAD

~

One day I went to dad and told him I was going to New York to practice, to fish a tournament in the Thousand Islands.

"Pops, you have to see what bass fishing is like up there," I said. "It is fantastic."

So he rode up with me and we fished together. On the final practice day I said, "Dad, put on a spinner bait. We're going to thump them today."

But dad wanted to use a slower bait. He tied on a G-4 tube bait.

The first cast I caught a three-pound smallmouth.

"Dad, you need to be throwing a spinner bait."

But he was relaxing in the back of the boat, smoking, sitting back, having fun with his tube bait.

I caught four fish that day.

Dad caught 14.

It was not until the end of the day that I realized what was going on. We were fishing in clear water, and the fish saw me in the bow of the boat throwing my spinner bait. They weren't biting often, but they were curious. They stayed out on the edge of visibility then fell in behind the boat, looking and watching. And there's dad sitting down, dragging his tube bait, and catching them behind the boat.

That was a great day for him.

Other fishermen on the trail were getting to know him. They picked up the name Pops. Then I had a jacket made with his nickname sewn on the front. It was not long before many of the best bass fishermen in the world were calling him Pops.

They brought him into their world and welcomed him, and he loved them.

THE BASS

~

I was fishing Lake Toho in central Florida, near the south end of Paradise Island, throwing a Johnson Spoon at a grass clump. As the bait descended, a bass leaped out of the water and ate it in midair.

Another time I threw a buzz bait, and before it hit the water a bass grabbed it.

This is such a stunning sight that many of us are momentarily struck with awe when it happens.

I've seen bass jump almost four feet straight up and pounce down on the bait like a cat on a mouse.

Bass love to jump. I've had bass jump into my boat. Once I heard a noise and looked around. A three-pounder had jumped into my boat while chasing a dragonfly.

Many species of fish, if threatened by a predator, will leap from the water. But the bass leaps more often than most.

The aerobatics of the bass make them the premier freshwater fish in America. It makes them the fish we love to pursue.

VERSATILITY

~

Some anglers specialize. They are world-class with jigs or flipping or skipping bait up under docks, using crank baits or top-water fishing.

When the fish are doing their thing, these anglers are competing against only four or five other anglers who specialize in the that same thing. And they can place high or win tournaments.

But when the fish are not doing their thing, specialists have a tough time on the water.

A top professional angler should have a specialty. But he must be versatile. He must know when, where, and how to throw a spinner bait. He must know how to use a jerk bait. He needs to know how, when, and where to fish with a Carolina rig. He must know his tackle box.

If you are versatile, you can compete under all conditions and hold on to your tournament standing.

That is how Rick Clunn had made it to the Classic for 25 consecutive years. No matter what the fish are doing, he can catch them. He is very, very good with a spinner bait, with a jig, with flipping and pitching. I don't know anything that Rick Clunn doesn't do well.

Versatility is the single greatest asset of a bass angler.

"Shaw is considered the best sight fisherman in the sport of bass fishing.... You have to know what to look for under all different conditions. Sometimes you see the bed—a white spot on a dark bottom—before you see the fish. Shaw can read all that.... Until I fished with Shaw, I was never a sight fisherman. I've been a professional angler almost 30 years, and I tend to fish other ways. I am much more experienced than Shaw, but when we fished together, the master became the student."

—Rick Clunn

FISHING WITH CHILDREN

~

I was fishing with Polly and my two children, Amy and Shaw-Shaw. He is Shaw Eric Grigsby, but we call him Shaw-Shaw. The four of us were on the east pass of the Suwanee River. Polly was reading. Amy was four and was casting with a child's rod.

I was using a new bait-casting reel that a manufacturer had asked me to test. It was one of a kind, not yet in production, and I loved it. I was using a single-piece rod, 6½-feet long, about a seven power with tremendous sensitivity. I was dragging a worm and could feel every nuance of the bottom. It was the best outfit I had ever used.

I was fishing the worm down a strip of eel grass when I felt a little tap. A bass had eaten the bait. I set the hook and handed Amy my brand new super rod and reel, and she reeled in a 13-inch largemouth.

She was proud of her fish and didn't want to release it immediately. So I put it in the live well. Amy and Shaw-Shaw had their heads down in the live well watching the fish when I got another bite, set the hook, and called for Amy to take the rod. She started reeling. I stood back relaxed, proud of my daughter and even more amazed at the rod and reel.

The fish was about ten feet from the boat when Amy suddenly went horizontal. The fish had seen the boat and exploded in the other direction. I had a split second of hesitation. Did I go for my daughter or did I go for that magic rod and reel?

I caught Amy by her life jacket as she cleared the edge of the boat, pulled her back, and stood her beside me. It was natural for a child to be frightened by such an experience. After all, a fish had almost jerked her overboard.

She was on the edge of tears but never turned loose of the rod. What a girl!

That's my daughter!

But that big bass was still out there and still fighting.

I knew that if Amy didn't land the fish, she probably would never fish with me again. She was a four-year-old who had suddenly discovered that bass fishing can be a contact sport.

"It's your fish, Amy."

"No."

"You can do it, Amy."

She sat back and reeled and reeled. I was holding on to her. She caught the bass. It weighed more than seven pounds—big for the Suwanee River.

It was a Kodak moment.

Shaw-Shaw once caught a 6½-pounder that almost took him out of the boat because I forgot that I had the drag locked down tight when I handed him the rod. He wasn't about to turn loose of that rod. If I hadn't released the drag, the fish would have pulled him into the water.

When you take your children fishing, don't be too serious. Let your children be children. If they want to swim around the boat or hang on to a rope while you tow them with the trolling motor, fine. A child's early fishing experiences should be fun. Save your serious fishing for when you are alone.

To this day when I come home after weeks on the road and ask my children what they want to do, chances are they both will say, "Let's go fishing."

I believe they will continue to fish after they become adults. And one day they will be married and will continue to enjoy the sport—and will pass the joy of bass fishing on to their children.

NECESSITIES

~

No matter the conditions, hot or cold, rain or sunshine, calm or windy, there are two things I must have when I go on the water. Two necessities.

The first is polarized sunglasses, which I wear for several reasons.

One reason is safety. A bass could blow a plug and send it rocketing toward my face.

I also wear them for the polarization. I have the reputation of being one of the best sight fishermen on the tournament trail. A big reason for that reputation is polarized sunglasses, which enable me to see underwater. I often see fish that other fishermen miss. The third reason I wear them is to protect my eyes from ultraviolet rays.

I always carry two pairs. For everyday fishing and to give me good contrast when I am on the water, I wear a pair with brown lenses. The second pair has yellow lenses. I wear them early in the morning or during inclement weather and to see details under the water. The extra punch they give my vision never ceases to amaze me.

I consider sunglasses crucial in my line of work, so I don't buy them off the rack at the corner drugstore. I wear the best I can get.

The second thing I consider a necessity out on the water is sunscreen. Before I get in my boat, I liberally apply a 30 SPF to my face, neck, and hands. I use it year-round. And even on the hottest days, I wear long pants and long-sleeved shirts. Many of the shirts are a tight weave with an SPF factor built into the fabric.

Some fishermen wear shorts and take off their shirts when they are on the water. They think it is unmanly to use sunscreen. But I am from central Florida, and today I can easily recognize the people I went to school with who were sun worshipers.

They look like prunes. And many of them have had melanomas removed from their bodies. I believe in taking care of my body. I have only one.

THE BASS

~

I will always enjoy the challenge of the largemouth. But in some ways the smallmouth is more exciting. He is ferocious—a tiger of a fish.

I was fishing a tournament on Lake Champlain, up on the Canadian border between New York and Vermont. This clear lake is one of the most beautiful and historic bass lakes in the country. I was fishing almost under the shadow of Fort Ticonderoga.

The practice days were some of the best I ever had with smallmouth. Every day I hooked fish weighing up to six pounds, which is big for a smallmouth.

I thought when the tournament began I was going to have some great days.

What a surprise was in store.

The first day I caught two fish weighing a total of four pounds.

No matter how well you do in practice, no matter how good you think you are, no matter how great your technical knowledge or how versatile your technique, there are days when it is all for nought. Nothing works.

You and everything you think you know are rejected by the bass. You must understand this.

How you handle these times reveals much about your character.

Bass fishing is a mental game. When you decided to become a bass fisherman, you picked a sport that has the potential to humiliate you. Frequently.

Don't hold on to the bad days. Don't go into a slump.

During the next two days of the tournament on Lake Champlain, I caught limits of three-pounders. I salvaged the tournament and earned the points to maintain my standing for the Classic.

Learn and progress.

You'll have bad days not only in bass fishing but in life.

However, bass fishing provides more of these days than does life.

SIGHT FISHING

~

If you ask the pros on the tournament trail who is the best sight fisherman around, they will give you my name.

Here's what I know about sight fishing.

Sight fishing combines two sports: hunting and fishing. Hunting because you have to stalk a fish that at first you might not be able to see. You might see a boil in the water, a swirl, a shadow.

When I am sight fishing, I use light equipment: a spinning reel with 10-pound test line. I find that I get more strikes when I use green line. Green line blends with the vegetation. And water, even when it is clear, usually has a greenish or bluish tint.

When you are sight fishing, put the sun behind you. This greatly increases your ability to see fish underwater.

If you want to talk to someone in the boat, whisper.

Sound travels well under water.

If you want to move around in the boat, do so gently.

The bass can feel the vibration on his lateral lines.

Wear natural colors, earth tones, which allow you to blend in with the background and make you less visible.

The bass sees movement.

Once I was fishing and saw a four-pounder. "Throw on that bass," I whispered.

When my partner drew his arm back to cast, the bass spooked.

Bass are extraordinarily sensitive to movement, especially movement from above. Remember, they have been hunted by other fish and birds and by fishermen since they were fry.

Crouch and use side casts.

In clear water the bass feeds by sight. The bait has to look good.

Downsize your bait. If it is too big, it doesn't look like what bass eat in clear water. Shad and crawfish colors are good because that's what the bass likes to eat.

Many anglers think of sight fishing only in the spring, when bass go shallow to spawn. But if the water is clear, you can sight fish much of the year. Even after a heavy rain, when the upper end of a lake is muddy, the lower end often remains clear. And a lake with a lot of underwater vegetation to filter out the silt remains clear most of the time.

Winter is the limiting factor in sight fishing because bass tend to go deeper in winter. But even then, if the water is clear, you can sight fish. You can look deep underwater and see bass hunkered around a point.

Sight fishing intimidates many bass anglers. There are incredibly versatile anglers out there who are reluctant to add sight fishing to their list of techniques. They believe if a bass sees the angler, the bass will reject whatever bait is offered.

And some anglers think water can be too clear for fishing.

I don't.

Tire Bass

~

One of the most unusual bass out there is the tire bass.

Tractor tires and truck tires and car tires are sometimes seen underwater. This is not a good pattern to fish because there are not that many tires out there.

But when you see tires, fish them.

A tire provides a big hole, shelter, and cover—all of which are prized by the bass.

A tire bass usually is a big bass.

Knots

~

At fishing seminars most pros never talk about knots.

They think the subject is too basic, that you are there to learn how to find and catch bass.

I talk about knots in every seminar I teach. And afterward, when anglers gather around for questions, invariably the thing most of them want to talk about is knots.

In bass fishing I use only three knots.

The Double Improved Clinch.

The King Sling.

The Palomar.

The Improved Clinch is the most common knot used by fishermen. It is a good knot, but it is only 80 percent knot strength. That means if you tie this knot on a 10-pound test line, the knot reduces it to 8-pound test. Then you have the water absorption factor common in monofilament, which further reduces the strength.

THE PALOMAR KNOT

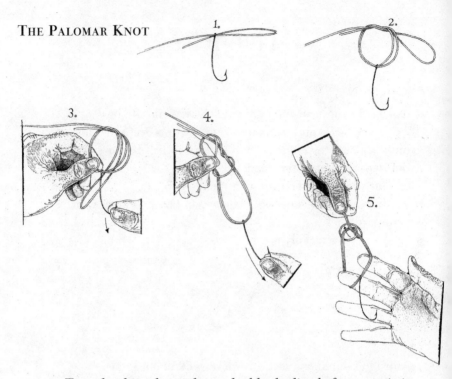

To make this a better knot, double the line before you tie it. That makes it a Double Improved Clinch and raises the knot strength to almost 100 percent.

Paul Elias taught me the King Sling. I use it with top-water baits. Some crank baits and jerk baits come with a split ring on the eye of the bait. If I find that the split ring restricts the action, I take it off and tie a King Sling to give more action.

Let me tell you how strong this knot is.

I was doing a seminar and tied a King Sling to a top-water bait. After the seminar I clipped the line above the knot and tossed the bait back into my tackle box. A few days later I was shooting a television show and a sponsor asked if he could borrow my tackle box and go fishing. When he opened the box, the bait with the loop of the King Sling was on top. He thought this was a secret trick used by the pros, so he took the lure and tied his line through the loop and went out and caught three five-pounders. I couldn't believe it. But it showed how strong the knot is.

When properly tied, the King Sling is almost 100 percent knot strength.

The best knot is the Palomar. You probably know the knot. But I do something extra that makes all the difference. I add something you will not see in any knot book. At the end, after you drop the bait through the loop, make the loop flop over on top and create the knot before you cinch it tight.

This version of the Palomar does not lose strength when it's tied. It is 100 percent knot strength.

After a seminar in which I discuss knots, the Palomar is the one I am most frequently asked to demonstrate.

The Palomar can be used with any line. But if you are using braided line, a double Uni-knot is better.

Sometimes when you quickly cinch a knot, the monofilament line tends to burn a bit. So I always moisten the line and pull slowly. The moisture aids the knot in slipping into position. By pulling slowly, I prevent the burn.

The other pros are right. Knots are basic.

But the basics are crucial in bass fishing.

You must control everything that can be controlled because there are so many variables that are out of your control.

BACKLASH AND LINE TWISTS

At the beginning of a cast, a bait-casting reel always goes faster than the bait; then for much of the cast, the bait and the reel are traveling at the same speed. At the end of the cast, the bait begins to slow down and again the reel is faster.

A backlash can occur anytime the reel runs faster than the bait.

To prevent a backlash, hold your thumb lightly on the spool at the beginning of the cast.

Very lightly.

Loosen up as the bait flies through the air.

Use a light thumb again as the bait descends. Stop the line either a fraction of a second before the bait hits the water or at the instant it hits.

Even the most experienced angler occasionally has a backlash.

Watch how an experienced angler and an inexperienced angler handle the problem.

The inexperienced angler is impatient. He grabs a handful of line and jerks. He tries to force the backlash loose.

Then you hear him talking about how he hooked a fish and it broke the line.

That's because jerking on a backlash nicks the line and weakens it.

Knowing how to clear a backlash will enable you to bring more fish to the boat.

Here's how an experienced angler does it.

First, *before you pull the line*, place your thumb firmly on the spool. Tighten the drag down all the way. With your thumb still held tightly on the spool, turn the reel handle one or two revolutions. This tightens the line from underneath. Then push the free spool and clear the loop formed by the backlash. Finally, return the drag to its normal position.

Don't use strength to clear a backlash.

Use finesse.

Now for line twists.

Out on the water you have seen a brother angler casting a spinning reel. And occasionally you see him lean over the reel and hear his language turning the air blue.

The line has twisted and looped.

That's a line twist.

A line twist is to a spinning reel what a backlash is to a

bait-casting reel. It is caused by several factors. A combination of light bait and heavy line can mean that as the bait is retrieved, the line is spooled on loosely. One way to prevent this is to put the top of the rod near the surface of the water after every cast. This keeps the line in the water and causes more tension, thus making the line go onto the spool more tightly.

Another factor is a bait that spins as it is retrieved. And a third is reeling when a fish is pulling the drag out.

Freeing a line twist can be so frustrating that it can make you want to hold the rod like a harpoon and see how far you can throw it across the water.

Here's a simple technique that will prevent having a problem with line twists.

After you make the cast and click over the bale, simply seize the line just above the reel and give it a light tug. It takes longer to describe than it takes to do it.

Make this a habit. Practice until you do it without thinking. Cast.

Tug.

You will have no more line twists.

CONTROL

~

An angler, if he is thoughtful and methodical and prudent, can control many aspects of bass fishing.

He can buy the best available rods, reels, lines, and lures. He can buy a good boat with state-of-the-art electronics and a strong dependable trolling motor. He can make sure his knots are tight and his hooks are sharp. He can study the weather and the water and the bass.

But there is much about fishing he cannot control.

Or he thinks he cannot. Which is the same thing.

Many anglers believe they have little control over what happens after the bait hits the water.

When will the bass strike?

Where will he strike?

How will he hit it?

Will he inhale the bait or will he barely be hooked?

What will he do once he has the bait in his mouth? Will he jump or will he run? Will he go deep? Will he break off the line on a piling?

What will he do when he sees the boat?

I know an angler, one of the best in the country, who is not very good at landing fish. He can hook them. But afterward he controls neither the fish nor the situation. He loses a lot of fish.

He compensates for his lack of technical skills by hooking so many fish that it doesn't matter if he loses some.

I rarely get on huge amounts of fish. But I land almost every one I hook.

By controlling what happens after the fish bites, you eliminate more variables. And you bring more fish to the boat.

Try to keep the bass from changing directions. After the strike and when the bass realizes he is hooked, he runs straight. Let him run. If he runs through heavy cover, let him run.

If you pull hard when he is running, you will turn him either left or right. When he changes directions, he can wrap the line around a piece of cover. If this occurs, three things can happen: He can break off, he can get slack line and blow the hook, or he can rotate the hook and lose it.

Keep the fish in view so you can react instantly to what he is doing.

When you are fighting the fish, fight the fish. By that I mean that you should not try to land a fish while opening the live well or flipping switches on the boat. If you are not paying attention and he jumps, he is gone.

Keep him underwater where there is a lot of resistance. Stick the rod down in the water until the reel is barely above the surface. Keep the bass down.

Sometimes the fish comes to the surface or runs near the boat, and you notice he is barely hooked. Play him accordingly. You don't want this fish to jump. If he goes airborne, he will toss the hook.

Don't relax when the fish approaches the boat. Getting him close doesn't mean you are about to boat him; it means that when he sees you, no matter how tired he is, he almost certainly will make a final effort to escape. Chances are he will jump.

A thousand times I've had fish jump when they came near the boat. Expect him to try it.

If it is a small fish, you can boat-flip him. If he is too big for that, lead him around in figure-eights until he is tired. Then grab him by his lower lip and put him in the boat.

Watch the fish.

Watch the line.

Control the variables.

Control is especially important when you are using light line.

Almost every time an angler catches a bass, he hauls back hard and winches the fish toward the boat. From the moment the bass is hooked, the angler turns the experience into a test of strength between him and the fish.

This is a common technique when using heavy line. Even the pros do it.

But fighting the bass doesn't work with light line. The only technique that consistently works is not to fight when the bass is fighting and, conversely, to fight when the bass is not fighting. I've won three B.A.S.S. tournaments on Sam Rayburn, and each win involved big fish on light line.

Here's why this technique works.

Bass are among the most unpredictable creatures in the

world. But in one or two things, they are absolutely predictable.

First, if you hook one and he runs, he will run straight for no more than 40 feet.

Second, after this burst of speed, he stops. He is used to ambushing his dinner and he is tired. He also is disoriented. He has to catch his breath and figure out what's going on.

When he runs, let him run. He is pulling against the drag. Don't try to horse him into the boat.

When he stops, bear down and crank fast, leading him back in the same direction he came from.

It's okay if a bass runs through heavy cover.

If he makes a second run, let him go. He will tire out before the drag does. When he stops, you start cranking again.

This technique means you are doubling up on him: When he runs he is fighting the drag, and when he stops you are cranking.

This technique will significantly increase the number of bass you put in the boat.

RELAX

~

I was fishing Rayburn and I was on fish. I was catching them on jigs and I was bagging them, catching four- and five-pounders like they were going out of style. I was living large and loving life. This was going to be a great tournament.

When the tournament began, I was tighter than a rubber band. I was so keyed up with expectation that I was fishing like a wild man—casting and cranking, casting and cranking. Way too fast.

The first day I caught one bass.

If you blow the first day of a tournament, it is difficult to recover.

Knowing that made me fish even faster. I couldn't slow down.

I was overexcited and still fishing too fast. I caught a few fish the second day, but I was never in the running.

And I thought I was going to win.

Since then I have seen this happen to young anglers many times. There is tremendous pressure on them to produce, to make a check, to prove themselves.

I've seen young anglers burn through a pocket of fish without catching one, and then they leave without knowing that they've run away from a big pile of fish.

When you are on the water, relax. Have nothing but fishing on your mind. Don't think about the bills you have to pay. Don't think about it being two hours to weigh-in. Don't think about the fish you saw another angler catch.

Listen. Accept what you hear from the wind and the sunlight and the water. Be open to all that is going on around you.

Be in tune with the bass.

RULES

~

Rules guide the conduct of the angler. Tournament promoters print the rules, give copies to the contestants, and even announce many of the rules at registration.

But the unwritten rules, the ones never announced, are the most important rules in bass fishing. And they apply each time you go on the water. We have lived by these rules and fished by these rules from the beginning.

Rule Number One. On the first day of a tournament if you draw a partner who is on fish, you don't go back to his spot the second day and fish with your next partner. You don't go back unless he invites you. He owns those fish.

Thou shalt not steal.

But you can utilize his knowledge. If he is throwing Carolina rigs on a point, you can throw Carolina rigs on other points.

I was fishing a tournament on Buggs Island and I was thumping them on a spinner bait. The second day I was paired with an angler from Minnesota. I caught five that went to almost 25 pounds and was in the lead. My partner came to me that day after weigh-in and I gave him the spinner bait I was using. He said, "I don't want to fish any place you are going to fish. Where can I go that won't bother you?"

I told him to go farther up the same creek, that I was stopping at a point. "You know the pattern. Use it and go fishing."

He did the sporting thing. And he came in the next day with a 19-pound stringer, one of the biggest he ever caught.

Rule Number Two. When you are in the boat with another angler, you don't throw on your partner's fish. Sometimes the angler gets a bite and misses the fish. The fish is still there, wondering what's going on, searching and hunting and saying, "Where'd it go? Where'd it go?"

The fisherman who first got the bite owns the fish. The partner in the boat does not go after that fish unless invited to do so.

Rule Number Three. If you are paired with a fisherman who is among the top ten contenders, a man who has a good shot at winning the tournament, don't hinder his day. Give him his shot. There are not many opportunities to win a tournament.

Remember, we compete against the bass. Not each other.

Rule Number Four. If a fisherman is fishing a bank, don't pull in on him. The written rule is that if he is anchored and his trolling motor is out of the water, you can't fish within 50 yards. The unwritten rule is that if he is fishing a point, you don't pull in on his point. If he is in a pocket, stay out of his pocket, even if there is room for another boat in there.

If he is fishing a bank, let him have it. You can go down 300 or 400 yards and fish back toward him. Or you can pull in behind him and fish back the way he came. But don't pull in a few feet from him and fish that bank.

The legends in this business, Guido Hibdon, Denny Brauer, Rick Clunn, all have tremendous respect for fellow competitors. If they round a point and see an angler in a cove, they turn around they don't fish that cove. They go elsewhere.

B.A.S.S. has always held anglers to the very highest standards of sportsmanship. In a B.A.S.S. tournament, if there is any doubt about a possible rule violation, the angler takes a polygraph. Every angler signs a paper agreeing to the polygraph.

But on the new tournament trails starting up today, some young fishermen are not following the rules. Most violations of the unwritten rules come from beginners who are not taught good sportsmanship. They don't know the unwritten rules; or they are aggressive and feel the need to get that check. They do things that they probably wouldn't do after a few years of professional fishing.

This is a sport where you get money if you come in second, third, fourth, or tenth. When your chance comes to win, you want that to be in your hands, you want to be able to control your destiny and not have it influenced by someone else.

What these young anglers don't understand is that the more unsportsmanlike they are, the more they will experience unsportsmanlike behavior. It will all come back to them.

The unwritten rules are simple. They all come down to respect.

Respect a man's water.

Respect a man's fish.

"Shaw and I were fishing the same area, but Shaw was on a point and I was fishing the grass, not nearly as deep as he was fishing. Shaw had his limit and I had not caught a keeper all day....It was about an hour and a half before weigh-in and Shaw said, "Come on out here and let me show you how to line up on this point....Not many fisherman would give up their spot....It saved my skin. I would not have made a check if it hadn't been for Shaw, and I might not have qualified for the BASS Masters Classic....Most fisherman won't hurt a competitor; they won't do anything underhanded. But they won't go out of the way to give them a spot. It's like giving your competitor a fish. Even among the best of friends fishing on the tour, that happens very seldom....Shaw is a very intense individual when it gets down to competition. He is there to do business. But he lives by the Golden Rule. If we all lived by the Golden Rule, it would be a better world."

—Mark Davis

TIP

~

I've said bass are curious and are drawn to noise. A bait that makes a small, consistent noise will get their attention, and the bass will come in for a close look.

That's why rattles are so popular on jigs.

But jigs with hard-mounted rattles are expensive. Sometimes they break off.

And not all jigs come with rattles.

If you have a jig you like, and it has no rattle, here's how to make an inexpensive rattle jig that will not break. (And it will bring the extra satisfaction that comes from making a bait yourself. Dad was right about that.)

Take a piece of surgical tubing one inch long and insert a rattle in each end. Then push a hook through the middle of the tubing and slide it under the skirt of the jig.

Simple as that.

It will not break—how can you break surgical tubing?

It performs well and it doesn't impede the hook set.

The bass hears the noise and zeroes in on it.

The rattle is most effective in stained or muddy water and in vegetation.

JIG AND PIG

~

Denny Brauer and Tommy Biffle love to flip a jig.

That is their specialty, and it is a good one to have. The jig has been around forever, won a lot of tournaments, and can be used all year long.

The jig is simply a lead head on a hook with an attached rubber skirt. The pig comes in when you attach a piece of pork to the end of the bait. A piece of pork looks good on a hook. Bass like the salt and the texture, and once they get a piece of pig in their mouths, they want to eat it.

But pork has two problems.

It dries out quickly once it is exposed to air.

And when the bass strikes, the pork sometimes folds over the hook. This means that when the angler sets the hook, he doesn't drive the hook through the pork and therefore doesn't hook the fish.

So today most anglers use plastic rather than pork. It doesn't dry out and is injected with salt and scents to make it smell and taste like pork. Technology is amazing.

If I'm using a jig and pig, I usually start with plastic, and if it doesn't do well, I change to pork. There are times when pork will catch bass when plastic will not.

I will always have pork in my boat.

FEELING THE BOTTOM

~

It is common knowledge that the bass likes to hide in places that may be visible to the angler: laydowns, lily pads, grass lines, riprap. Visible cover.

But there is also invisible cover—underwater structure such as stumps, rock piles, channel edges, and underwater points.

Anglers believe that today's electronics are so good that all they need to know about the bottom can be found by looking at their sonar screens.

Yet some electronics can be deceptive.

A thick grass pile might trick your sonar into indicating you are over a brush pile. But if you drag a Carolina rig through it, you know by the feel that it is grass.

The bass loves thick grass.

I am a great believer in electronics. When I am looking for fish, I always use the electronics first.

But I also use my bait to feel and know the bottom.

SCENTS

~

Commercially available scents smell like old crawfish or dead fish. Pretty bad stuff. But bass like it, and I always carry a can in my boat.

Some anglers wonder if the scents are effective. But I have tossed a bait three or four times at a bass without getting a strike. Then I sprayed the bait with scent, and the bass hit it the next cast.

I know scents work. A bass has a powerful sense of smell and a well-developed sense of taste.

You might have seen bass bumping a surface lure. Fisheries experts think the bass may be tasting the lure. That's one reason lures impregnated with salt are effective. The bass likes the taste and will sometimes hold it in his mouth.

Baits dipped in a scent don't attract bass from a long distance. And the lures don't leave a long odor trail; instead, they leave little puddles of odor.

Not only are these scents appealing to bass, they cover odors that might be on the hands of the angler: gas, oil, or sunscreen. Bass have a strong aversion to sunscreen. All traces must be washed off or covered with scents before handling baits or lines.

I use scents often on slow baits.

Scents are not important on spinner baits and crank baits because these baits move so fast. But you can still use scents. They may help the fish to track the bait and aid in his decision about whether or not to bite.

TIP
~

You will occasionally snag your bait on an underwater log, heavy brush, or in the crevasse of a rocky bottom.

It happens to every angler.

Don't lean back and use brute force to jerk the bait free. This usually sets the hooks deeper or wedges the lure tighter.

If it does free the bait, the next thing you see will be treble hooks zooming for your face.

When you snag your bait, finesse it.

Here's how.

Hold the rod at about eleven o'clock. Put your thumb on the reel and hold the line as tightly as possible. At the same time, use the other hand to seize the line between the lowest guide and the reel. Pull out several feet of line. Raise the tip of the rod until the line is as taut as a guitar string.

Then simultaneously release the line in your hand and drop the rod tip toward the snagged bait.

Monofilament stretches. If you perform this technique correctly, the stretched line snaps like a rubber band and pops the snagged hook loose. It works underwater as well as on top of the water.

You must understand the concept. If you release the line in your hand and don't drop the rod, the line remains taut at the tip of the rod. You have to simultaneously release your hand and drop the rod.

It usually works. It's not 100 percent effective.

But then, few things are.

FOLKLORE AND SECRETS

~

Too much folklore has accumulated about bass fishing. Much of the folklore has achieved biblical weight even though it is wrong.

For instance, one of the best known axioms of bass fishing is that 90 percent of the fish are in 10 percent of the water. It's called the compression concept, and anglers take it to mean that most bass are close to the shoreline.

David Fritts proved this wrong when he won a half-million dollars in one year by turning his back to the shore and fishing offshore structure—the ledges and drop-offs instead of bushes and laydowns. He moved up into the million-dollar-winner category of anglers because of his skill at deep cranking.

Ninety percent of the fishermen on a given body of water are up near the bank fishing for what they think are 90 percent of the fish. These anglers must not know about all the fish offshore.

I think maybe 50 percent of the fish are on the bank and 50 percent in open water.

This is a difficult concept for anglers because when they turn their backs on the bank, they are looking away from what they see and know; they're looking toward what they can't see and don't know.

When an angler looks offshore, he has to visualize the underwater structure.

Offshore, it is more difficult to present the bait and to know what the bait is doing.

And the angler has to make multiple casts to cover invisible structure. He might spend a day finding one good spot where fish are stacked up.

The learning curve associated with offshore fishing intimidates a lot of anglers.

But once you master it, the amount of fish you can catch is amazing. And once you get on them in open water, you usually have them pretty much to yourself.

Question all folklore about the bass.

You will become a better fisherman.

Another bit of folklore is worth mentioning.

It is said that bass like wood next to weeds.

Translated, that means that weeds are the favorite structure of a bass and that laydowns and stumps are a close second.

If you have been bass fishing for any length of time, you have heard and dutifully noted this bit of wisdom.

You go out on the water, and in the back of your mind you're hearing, "Bass like wood next to weeds."

But this is true only part of the time. It depends on the time of year. In the winter, as the water cools down, or in the early spring, when bass are thinking of spawning, they prefer rocks to either wood or weeds because rocks hold heat. So, for much of the year, you will find more bass on rocks than you will on wood.

When weeds deteriorate in the fall, fish move away. They could move to wood or they could move to rocks.

There are few absolutes in bass fishing.

Everything is relative to the conditions at the time you are on the water.

The accuracy of folklore also depends on location.

For instance, Lake Okeechobee in southern Florida has no stumps or laydowns in the main body of the lake. So don't look for wood. But there are weeds. And North Carolina lakes often have lots of laydowns. But sometimes there are not many weeds.

When you go after the bass, you look over the water and you play the hand you are dealt. Until you see the cards, until you are on the water, you can't say what you will do.

So don't always say, "I'll go for wood and weeds." It might

work once or twice and then you will have to adjust. Fishing is a game of choices and adjustments.

Think of weeds and wood as primary cover.

But whether or not fish are there depends on the lake and the time of year.

A final word on folklore.

It is widely believed that creek mouths, the place where a creek dumps into a river or lake, is a place where bass can always be found.

Some anglers believe creek mouths are the mother lodes of bassdom—the single best place to find fish.

But there is no place where bass are found all the time.

Write that down.

Say it over and over to yourself as you go to sleep so you won't forget it.

There is no place where bass are found all the time.

Bass are migratory. And they move around within their migratory patterns. If their food moves, they move. Remember, the most important thing to a bass is food. They will put up with a lot of unpleasant conditions if food is present.

Every day on the water is a new day.

Just as there is too much folklore about bass fishing, there are too many secrets—unnecessary secrets.

We have too many anglers who think their knowledge of fishing has a top-secret security classification and that other anglers are trying to steal their secrets. They believe if they keep everything secret that they will catch fish no one else can catch. They even believe if other anglers know their secrets, those anglers will come in and wear out the fish. If you meet these anglers on the water, either they won't tell you anything about where the fish are biting or they will deliberately mislead you.

What they forget is that an angler has to relocate the fish almost every time he goes on the water. One time the water level is up and the fish are inside; a week later the water level might be down and the fish are outside. Another week later, the water is muddy and the fish have moved again.

Simply because an angler catches fish at one place this week doesn't mean he can do the same next week.

I have won three tournaments on Rayburn, and each time I caught my stringers in different places.

Unless I am fishing a tournament, I don't mind telling another angler which bait I am using and the depth I am fishing.

The problem with passing along information is not that the other angler will catch all your fish; the problem is that when you tell another angler where the fish are and what they are biting, you are keeping that angler from developing his own knowledge and his own pattern.

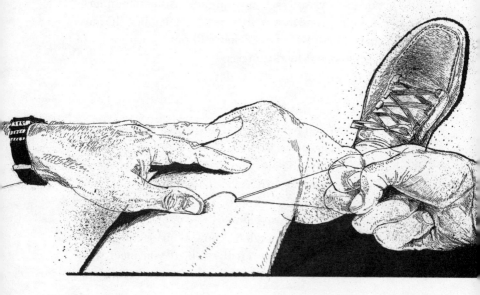

The best thing for any angler is to figure out the pattern on his own.

That way he becomes a better fisherman.

HOOKED

~

I was fishing a tournament on the St. Johns River near Palatka, Florida, when my plastic worm snagged a dock. I made the mistake I have cautioned you about.

I tried to muscle it loose. I tugged until the line was stretched like a rubber band. Suddenly the worm broke free, and the 4/0 hook came toward me like a missile. I never had the time to move. The hook buried itself in a tendon in my arm.

It was too deep to pull out, and I couldn't push it through. So I cut the hook about halfway down the shaft, fished the remainder of the day, then had the hook cut out by a doctor.

Sooner or later you will find a hook imbedded in your skin. Most often it will be in your hand, arm, or leg; occasionally in the face or neck.

If the barb is embedded in cartilage or near an eye, or if no other method works, do not hesitate in getting off the water and seeking a doctor. You will need the doctor to cut it out.

But you can remove most hooks yourself and keep on fishing.

Many fishermen have a standard method for removing a hook: They push it through the flesh until the barb reemerges, use a pair of pliers to cut off the barb, then back the hook out.

This damages tissue and it hurts.

Here's a method that is quick, painless, and minimizes tissue damage. It's called the string method.

First, if it is a single hook, cut the line. The hook in your flesh should be clear. It's bad enough to have the hook in your flesh without a rod and reel attached to the other end. If it is a double or treble hook, cut everything loose except the offending hook and eye. If you must cut the top of the offending hook, cut it as high up the shaft as possible.

Then loop a double or triple strand of heavy line under the hook. Get a good grip on the line and hold it close to the flesh. Press down firmly on the eye of the hook; press it into your flesh so the gap of the hook is arced into the air.

Then jerk hard on the line so that the hook is backed out of the wound.

Make sure no one is behind you because the hook will rocket through the air. You don't want to plant it in someone else.

If you look at a hook from the side, you will see why this method causes the least pain. When you jerk hard on the line, you are pulling against the long curve of the hook. The curve shields and makes way for the barb and prevents additional damage to the flesh.

Next time you're hooked, try it.

TOURNAMENTS AND LOCALS

~

No matter what part of the country a tournament is held, local anglers are usually defeated by fishermen from other parts of the country.

That's because the local fisherman knows what he always does to catch bass in that lake. He has a history on that water. He sees a spot and he says to himself, "I caught a stringer there two years ago." He will fish that spot every time he passes.

The pro has no local knowledge. He doesn't drive by a spot and remember he caught a stringer there last year.

He finds out where the fish are located. He figures out what they are biting. Then he takes what he has learned and develops a pattern. He applies the pattern to the lake. He fishes places overlooked by locals.

Local fishermen take pride in saying, "I know the lake."

A pro says, "I know the fish."

Put another way, the local fisherman is often a spot fisherman. A pro is a pattern fishermen.

A pro listens to the water.

A pro listens to the fish.

'TATER BOATS

~

Some pros call them 'tater boats—boats operated by spectators at fishing tournaments. The boats and their owners may have driven hundreds of miles to be at a tournament so they can follow the pros around. They want to know where their heroes fish and what baits they use. They want to watch the techniques.

The spectator gallery for a big tournament has no equal in professional sports. In bass fishing, it is impossible to separate the fans from the middle of the action: There are no fences or security officers out on the water; no crowd control.

The spectator boats lie offshore from the launch site. Waiting.

At the Classic, a top pro may have up to 80 boats following him around the lake. The drivers have video cameras, binoculars, and tape recorders. They also have GPS so they can mark every spot where the pro catches a fish.

When two big-name fishermen happen to be fishing across the lake from each other and 25 or 30 boats are watching each fisherman, if one of the contestants decides to move on, a lot of boats suddenly converge.

If the pro is fishing a dock and using finesse techniques, the wake of arriving and departing spectator boats seriously interferes with his fishing.

At the end of the day when it is time to go to weigh-in, we time our arrival at the dock to the minute. We want to stay on the water as long as possible without being penalized for being late. Sometimes spectator boats congregate around the finish line.

I don't have a problem with the spectator boats. In fact, I enjoy them. Some of the operators I see year after year. I've gotten to know them and we always speak and joke around. They are fishermen and fans. And it is flattering that they come so far just to watch us fish.

But there can be problems. Sometimes the spectators don't understand that while this is a lot of fun for them, it is our livelihood. Our tournament standings and our careers are at stake. Spectators can cost us a lot of money.

Spectators cost Paul Elias the Classic one year. He was fishing a hump in the James River in Virginia when a spectator boat pulled up close by and the people in it started fishing.

He was very nice. He said, "Look, folks. I'm fishing the Classic, and I'm in position to win. So I'd really appreciate it if you let me have this spot for one more day. Then it will be all yours."

"Sure," the driver said. And he pulled off.

Paul left early in the afternoon for weigh-in. When he came back the next day, there was nothing. He didn't get a bite. A spectator came up and said, "After you left yesterday, those people you were talking to went back in there and caught about 30 fish."

They cost him the Classic.

Most people don't qualify every year for the Classic. And if a spectator comes in and takes the pro's fishing spot, he could prevent the pro from winning this all-important competition.

For spectators it's all a lot of fun.

For the pros, it's much more. If we don't catch fish, we don't feed our families.

But all we can do is hope the fans respect our water.

TEN-POUNDERS

~

I've been referring to bass as "he." But male bass are wimps. Fisheries experts say the male bass rarely grows bigger than about six pounds. It is the female that grows beyond ten pounds.

Catching a ten-pounder is like breaking par on the most difficult golf course in the country. It is a major landmark in the progression of a bass fisherman.

A ten-pounder shows why these fish are called largemouths: A big man can double both fists and easily slide them into the mouth of a ten-pounder.

It is folklore among anglers that bass don't get that big by being dumb.

That bit of folklore is absolutely true.

A ten-pounder is smart and cautious and has refused to eat a lot of baits. If she wasn't, she would have been caught when she was four or five pounds. By getting this large, she has beaten all the odds by staying disease free and healthy. Almost always she is a solitary fish and is much more territorial. Because she is so big—fish this size are called sows—she is not aggressive in chasing bait. She is cautious and discriminating, and she waits until it is so close, she can lunge a foot or so and swallow it. She often lives in an area difficult for an angler to approach. She has an uncanny knack at distinguishing between live food and artificial baits. A lot of learning is incorporated in a fish that big.

I caught ten over ten in one year: ten bass weighing over ten pounds, all from Orange Lake near my hometown. It was very special for me.

The biggest bass I ever caught weighed 13 pounds 5 ounces. I caught it on a four-inch tube bait. When I close my eyes, I can still see the lily pads shaking and the intense swirls in the water as the fish swallowed my bait.

Big bass behave differently from other bass. Some studies show that they suspend in the daytime and become active at night. But my friend Doug Hannon, "The Bass Professor," has caught more than 500 bass weighing more than ten pounds, probably more than anyone else in the world; and he says almost all of them were caught in shallow water, and that 90 percent of them were caught between 10 a.m. and 3 p.m.

The question is: Do ten-pounders behave differently because they are ten-pounders, or are they ten-pounders because they behave differently?

I don't know. But here are some ideas about catching them.

A jig or a crawfish is a good bait for heavy cover.

Crank baits are good in open water. So are big plastic worms.

Catching a big one is a combination of the right presentation and working the bait slowly. Big fish don't pounce on everything they see. You have to make the bait enticing. You never know when a ten-pounder will strike, so you have to be prepared all the time.

Be patient. Work the drops. Feel the bottom for structure. Ultimately you will find a place that feels good. Most of the big fish are caught by methodical and careful anglers who know what has to be done and are willing to spend the time doing it.

One of the big difficulties in going out and specifically fishing for ten-pounders is that we fish only artificial baits. When a bass chases live prey, the prey emits panic signals that are impossible for an artificial lure to duplicate. The big bass is smart enough and experienced enough to discriminate between an artificial lure and a live prey.

Even so, a talented angler can bring in a ten-pounder.

Use every bit of skill you possess in working the lure. Make sure your equipment is in top condition. Retie your knots frequently. Use the quietest approach possible. Use your drag.

When you go after ten-pounders, you have to do everything right.

And even then it might be years before you hook one.

If you hook one.

"After the first day of competition, a leader board is established; and on the second or third day, if you go to a spot where one of the leaders is fishing, you show respect and you don't encroach on this area. You leave him alone....It was the first day of the tournament and I was fishing a hundred-yard stretch of shoreline....It was big enough that Shaw could have fished it without violating the rules. And I couldn't have been upset with him. But when Shaw saw I was fishing there, he never dropped his trolling motor. He never made a cast on that spot, even though he knew there was a huge concentration of bass there. He found another place to fish. I won that tournament by four ounces. If Shaw had fished there, he would have caught some of the fish I caught and I would not have won."

—Jay Yelas

PATIENCE

~

It happened on Lake Minnetonka outside Minneapolis.

I was Carolina rigging, dragging a lizard on a grass point, when a 1½-pounder hit me. I was reeling it in when suddenly something else, something much bigger, came on the line and started dragging and pulling and yanking.

I looked down, and there in the clear water I saw that a 4½-foot muskie had grabbed my bass.

The bass was sideways in the muskie's mouth. The hook was in the corner of the bass's mouth. If the muskie had eaten the bass, I could have set the hook and caught the muskie too. As it was, I pulled the muskie up to the edge of the boat before he spit out my bass. The bass had been in the muskie's mouth two or three minutes, and he'd been chewed on and dragged around.

I was going to reach down and hold him a moment until he recovered, then release him.

But the bass suddenly realized he was free. He jumped, threw my hook, and swam for the bottom.

The muskie was swimming away, heard the splash, spun around, and ate the bass.

If the bass had only been patient, he would have been okay. He would have lived.

We should learn from that.

The worst tournaments I have are when I forget what I know about being patient; when I try to force things to happen on my time rather than on bass time.

If there is a golden key to bass fishing—a single secret that, once understood, would almost instantly make us better anglers—it is that we must allow the bass to tell us what is going on in his world.

We cannot tell the bass what is going on. We cannot say, "This is what I'm giving you. Bite this spinner bait."

We have to sense the moods and the needs of the bass.

That is what fishing is all about. And we can do it only through patience.

Everything comes in time.

When you are on the water, patience is not only the most important thing, it is the only thing.

Just as it is in life.

WIND

~

One of the first things a professional angler does every morning during a tournament is tune the television in his room to the weather channel.

Not to find out if it will be hot or cold, sunny, cloudy, or rainy.

But for the wind.

The wind is the single most important weather factor we have to consider.

The direction and velocity of the wind determines where we fish, how we fish, or even if we fish.

Wind up to 10 miles an hour is of little consequence. From 10 to 20 miles an hour is marginal. But beyond 20, and the wind can ruin your day if you don't know how to handle it.

Wind does have a few benefits. It ruffles the surface enough that you can approach the bass without spooking him. Some disagree, but I think it pushes the baitfish into confined areas where bass often school up on them. It thrashes vegetation around and stirs up food for baitfish and, therefore, for bass.

The wind also creates currents in a lake, and currents cause bass to position themselves on points and at ambush spots.

Conventional wisdom dictates that anglers cast into the wind. One reason is because you won't drift down on the fish as you do if you cast downwind.

Throwing into the wind means numerous backlashes. Dial your reel up to five or seven and you will prevent some of these. You have to throw much harder when casting into the wind. This means you must be extra vigilant in controlling your thumb on the reel, especially when you release the bait at the beginning of the cast. And the wind causes the speed of the bait to decrease rapidly, so you must be prepared to use your thumb again.

A sidearm cast low to the water is more accurate and will keep the bait out of the major force of the wind.

Immediately after casting, put the rod tip down on the water to keep the wind from grabbing the line.

Casting into the wind calls for a high degree of both skill and concentration.

But this is not always the best strategy. And if the wind is above 20 miles an hour, it is virtually impossible to cast more than a few feet.

My rule of thumb is simple: If the wind is strong enough that I can't go against it with my trolling motor, I cast downwind.

I'm not sure it really matters whether you cast with the wind or against the wind; both methods still present the bait to the fish.

But you should avoid casting across the wind. This causes a huge bow in the line and makes it almost impossible to get a good hook set.

When the wind climbs above 20 miles an hour and waves start building, one of the most effective ways to fish is to take a spinner bait and work a bank. This is a straight-line approach to the bass. He hooks himself most of the time.

Fishing in high winds and doing so effectively is one of the angler's greatest challenges.

CANCER

~

The cigarettes finally got Pops.

In 1993 he was diagnosed with lung cancer.

The first thing the family wanted to know was how long he had to live. Doctors don't like to make such predictions, but his cancer was so advanced that doctors said his condition would become serious within a few months.

"Anything you want to do, we will do it," I told my parents. "If there is something unresolved with dad that he wants to resolve, something he did once that he wants to do again, a trip he wants to take, anything. Let's do it."

Dad knew he had only a short time to live, and the first thing he wanted to do was go back to Germany, where he had met my mom. So the whole family went to Germany. We had a wonderful time there. He went back to all his old haunts and told us of all the things he had done as a young man. He showed us streams where he had fished for trout long before I was born. The trip rejuvenated him.

When we returned, dad read a book about the power of prayer. It said prayer can make a difference to a sick person. The book didn't say the sick person would be cured, but it did say that he would get better. So the next time dad went with me to a tournament, he stood up at a meeting of Christian anglers and told them about his cancer.

"We'll pray for you, Pops," they told him.

Two years later, dad and I were still fishing together. He was growing older and he was more frail. But he was still fishing.

Our time on the water had brought us back together. Our relationship was repaired. We were again each other's best friend.

Dad was not reluctant to talk about his death. "If you are at a tournament when I die, don't come home," he said. He told me this in front of the entire family. "You don't need to be there for me. Fish the tournament. I know an angler's standing is decided by points. You can't afford to miss a tournament."

More than a dozen times out on the water, he turned to me and said, "Son, I don't want you to cry for me when I die. I've had a great life. I have a good wife, good children, and I was able to do so much in my younger days and, later, with my teaching. I had a full life. So don't cry for me."

But I did.

WEATHER

~

Bass anglers face their share of bad weather.

We regularly go out in weather that would keep the postman at home.

I fished a tournament on Logan Martin when it was snowing; the temperature was below zero, and the wind was blowing about 20 miles an hour.

At weigh-in that afternoon, Rick Clunn bounced up on the stage with the biggest sack of fish in the tournament. He looked out over the crowd of miserable shivering anglers and, with a big grin, said, "When I woke up this morning and looked outside, I knew I was going to catch a big sack of fish."

A guy standing next to me snorted, shivered, and said, "When I woke up this morning, I knew I was going to be a cold son of a gun."

I was struck by the difference in mental attitudes.

Rick knew he would catch fish. And he did. The other man knew he would be cold. And he was.

Later I fished a tournament on Grand Lake in Oklahoma.

The high during the day was 6°. Add in the chill factor from the water and the wind, and it was cold. The live wells were frozen shut. Bilge pumps would not work. The trolling motor froze in the down position, and I had to pour icy lake water on it to break it loose. Then it froze in the up position. The guide on my reel froze and would not move. Ice built up all over the boat. I had on two pairs of socks, thermal underwear, a ski bib, rain suit, and face shield—and I was still cold.

I didn't make a check in the tournament.

I took a long look at my own mental attitude and remembered how Rick Clunn dealt with extreme weather.

The next time I went to Grand Lake, I wanted miserable conditions. I prayed for cold and snow and sleet and misery.

My prayer was answered—and I fished. They were some of the worst conditions I have ever seen on the water.

I came in second in the tournament.

And I realized you have to have the right mindset before you can worry about the right hook set.

Bad weather keeps many fishermen out of a tournament. They are too worried about rain and snow going down their neck. When the weather really gets miserable, there are only a handful of roughies and toughies on the water.

Once I saw an angler who had been caught in a hailstorm come off the water. He had been able to protect his face with his hands, but the hailstones had hit his arms, giving him giant blood blisters and enormous purple bruises. He was battered.

But he fished through it all.

Tournaments are not called unless the weather is life-threatening. That rarely happens. But weather extreme enough to make life miserable out on the water happens frequently.

There are many places where I know the weather will be bad. Lake Ontario is always rough. Spring tournaments on Rayburn almost always have a day or so of extreme weather.

I've been caught out in 56-mile-an-hour winds and 8-foot

waves on the Potomac. It was so bad once on Santee Cooper in South Carolina, and the waves were so high, my partner's job was to look out for other boats that might run over us each time we crested a ten-foot wave.

Down in the troughs, stumps were all around us. If we had dropped off a ten-foot wave onto a stump, the boat would have been destroyed.

So we watched for other boats on the tops of waves and for stumps in the troughs.

I never look at adverse weather and say, "I'm not going to catch them when it's like this." In severe weather my confidence level pegs the meter. I know I am going to catch all the fish I want.

The bass are out there through it all.

So are we.

ON THE WATER

An angler's work is on the water.

During tournaments, we can't take off until safe light. But if we are fishing by ourselves, we have been known to ease out of the marina while it is still dark.

We like to be in our offices when the sun comes up.

Our offices change frequently. This week it might be a lake in Florida, next week a river in New York, and the next week an impoundment in Arizona. We tournament anglers fish all across America, from ocean to ocean and from border to border.

From our offices we rarely see or hear cars. And we might spend all day on the back of beyond without seeing another boat.

We do see bald eagles and osprey and coots and purple gallinules. We hear the soft and mournful cry of the loons. We see otters cavorting in the canals and beavers working in the creeks.

We see the sun break through early morning fog, and we see that brief moment after the sunrise when the air turns soft and pale. Artists refer to this moment as magic time, and they are right. We see lily pads turn up their soft green underbellies to a vagrant morning breeze. We see the noonday sun illuminate flowers of rainbow multiplicity in lakes all across the country. We see the blinding white-hot sunsets of summer and the soft purple sunsets of winter.

Throughout the day and throughout the year, we are at one with nature. We see a world as the world once was.

We have been on more of the ponds and lakes and rivers of America than most people even know about. And we know the most remote and secret and pristine regions of these waters.

We like our offices.

We don't want to see them changed.

THE FINAL FISHING TRIP

~

Dad was not doing well.

We could see he was going downhill.

He was having trouble breathing, and he had grown frail and was always tired. But each time we went fishing, he perked up. There was purpose in his life. He was renewed. Fishing rejuvenated him.

He always helped out at weigh-in. All his friends, the anglers who called him Pops, encouraged him. He had so many friends out on the trail.

I had my own television show, and I told him I wanted to tape a show with him and with my son—three generations of Shaw Grigsbys in the same boat.

"We'll call that show 'The Three Shaws,'" I said.

So we drove about an hour north of Gainesville to a series of lakes formed by phosphate mining. We were going to do a show about panfish.

Dad moved slowly and he had trouble getting in and out of the boat. But he was vintage Pops. He was an old Navy man and had the vocabulary to prove it. That day he talked about the importance of working for oneself and controlling one's own destiny.

"Be your own madam," he said. "Run your own whorehouse. Have everyone working for you."

Shaw-Shaw loved it. But I kept thinking that mine was a family TV show, and that some of this stuff would never get on the air.

It didn't. But Shaw-Shaw and I still remember it, and we still laugh about it.

That was the last fishing trip my dad and my son and I took together.

And it was one of the special days in my life.

GOODBYE

~

I was at a tournament on Lake Russell on the Georgia–South Carolina border when dad died. Polly didn't want me to hear of it from just anyone, so she tracked down Tim Tucker, a senior writer for *Bassmaster* magazine, who was a neighbor and close friend. He pulled me aside after weigh-in and said: "Pops is gone. He died early this morning."

I slumped against the wall and tears sprang to my eyes.

Tim stayed with me a few minutes and then left me alone to compose myself.

My one prayer throughout dad's illness had been, "Lord, be merciful to my dad." My prayer was granted. When dad died, he was not taking any pain medication. He spent his last evening singing songs with mom, hugging her, and remembering the old times. He went to sleep and didn't wake up.

I had to rush home to Gainesville. The next day I was supposed to be at Lake Hartwell on the Georgia–South Carolina border for another tournament.

The whole town of Elberton, Georgia, fell out for me that afternoon. A lieutenant in the sheriff's office was a bass fisherman, and he trailered my boat to his house. A tire on the trailer had a flat and he said, "I'll take care of it for you." Another angler then pulled my boat over to Hartwell so it would be there when I returned the next day.

All the fisherman knew and loved Pops. They were doing everything they could for him, and for his son.

Bass anglers are a close-knit group. We compete on the water, but when one of us is in trouble, the others rally around and do what needs to be done. We are family.

I drove to Atlanta and flew home to Gainesville. The funeral would not be for another week. I wanted to be with my family for that next week, but they knew about the tournament and insisted I return.

"You need to fish," mom said. "That's what he wanted. He told you many times what you should do when this happened."

So Sunday afternoon I flew back to Atlanta and drove to Hartwell.

The hardest thing I ever did was leave my family and go fishing.

Monday was a practice day. I was casting and crying. Casting and crying.

I had a week on the water dealing with dad's death before I returned home for his funeral. It gave me a lot of time to think about dad, about fishing, and about our relationship.

That was a tough tournament.

My dad had taught me to fish. Fishing broke us apart and fishing put us back together. Fishing made our relationship stronger than it had ever been. Some of the greatest days of my life were traveling to tournaments with my dad. We had almost ten years as fishing partners.

There were so many memories out on the water.

So many memories.

ESCAPE

~

One of the greatest things about fishing, the thing that makes it different from many other sports, is that there are so many levels of the game.

Fishing can supply whatever you need in your life.

It can be an escape.

And for those who want to sit in a boat and enjoy the sun and the water, and don't care whether they catch anything or not, fishing can be the ultimate relaxation—a slow and leisurely time of contemplation. Some people simply feel the ancient beckoning of the waters. They want to sit on a creek bank or in a boat and maybe cast a line or two.

Fishing can be entertaining. Take a look at a bunch of saltwater anglers if you want to see fishermen having a good time.

The challenge of improving our techniques can be totally consuming.

It can be a way to enjoy birds and animals and to observe all the mysteries of nature.

The lessons learned on the water can be carried back into life.

How you deal with adversity on the water tells much about how you deal with adversities during your lifetime.

Fishing can be anything you want it to be.

For a long time after my dad died, fishing was a place of renewal for me.

WATER

~

The first four tournaments I won were won by sight fishing—by seeing the fish, stalking them, and catching them.

That's how I became known as one of the best sight fishermen on the tournament trail.

Then I went to a B.A.S.S. tournament on Lake Sinclair in Georgia. It was in the spring. I remember because it was four months after Pops died.

In the spring, bass go shallow to spawn. I was hoping for another sight-fishing win when I got to Sinclair. Other fishermen thought the same thing. Every time conditions are right for sight fishing, anglers come up to me to talk, to remind me that this is my kind of water.

Conditions could not have been more different from what I was expecting. The tournament began shortly after a cold front had gone through and dumped tons of rain. Instead of being clear, the lake was high and muddy. For most bass fishermen, high and muddy is the worst of all possible combinations; it's bad enough to make them want to get off the water and go home and watch my TV show.

Remember what I said about being versatile.

I tossed out my game plan and started over.

High and muddy means new bushes and trees are submerged, making more cover for the bass. High and muddy tells you the bass will move on to the shallows to feed. High and muddy tells you they won't be able to see the bait until a split second before they strike.

The passage of the cold front tells you they will be lethargic and unwilling to chase food.

A bass has acutely developed senses. Through their lateral lines, they sense movement and vibration. They hear extraordinarily well.

High and muddy made me go to a spinner bait because it puts out flash and vibration. High and muddy made me use a bright color—chartreuse—not because bass know and like this color but because it allows them to see the bait easier in the stained water.

Passage of the cold front called for a very slow presentation.

My plan was for the bass to sense the vibration, move in to check out the noise, then see the flash of the blades and the bright color. I would slow roll the bait to give the bass all the time in the world to hear it, see it, and eat it.

When I went on the water I was nervous.

But my tactics were good.

I won the tournament.

That evening as I was packing up to leave, several anglers stopped by my room. My television show had aired that morning, but I had missed it because I was on the water. It was the episode I called "The Three Shaws."

"It was good to see Pops again," the anglers said.

I nodded in agreement.

It was good to have my dad there on the day I had a big win.

BOATS

~

If you always live though the experiences of others, you don't learn, grow, or change.

Which is one way of saying, there will come a time when you will want to buy your own boat. You don't want to fish from the bank forever. And you don't want to fish from the back of someone else's boat forever.

Having a boat allows you to find fish on your own rather than depending on your partner.

You gain self-confidence every time you find fish. You are more effective on the water.

Buying a boat means examining your priorities. Bass fishing can be a relaxing and relatively inexpensive hobby, or it can be an all-consuming and very expensive job. It can also be an obsessive undertaking. Many people who take up bass fishing as a hobby become caught in the sticky and almost unbreakable web of the fish's mystical spell. They become obsessed by the pursuit of the bass.

A boat enables you to fish new bodies of water. And it gives you the chance to learn what the fish are doing in lakes where you've never been. It gives you the chance to go to new lakes and new rivers and to figure out the fish on your own.

If your home water is a big impoundment, the next time there is a drawdown, or the next time the water is lowered to the winter pool, or the next time the water is lowered because of work being done on the locks, use your boat to study the lake. You can learn more about a lake when the water is low than you can in years of fishing; you can see cover and structure that ordinarily are invisible. If you've been catching fish on a spot and couldn't figure out why, go there at low water and take a look. Some anglers videotape their home lakes during drawdowns.

A boat opens up new worlds to an angler.

Buy a boat and move on up.

The bass boat business exploded in the late 1970s. Almost overnight, prices for a fully-rigged boat went from around $2,500 to around $5,000. And today a high-performance boat can cost in the mid-30s.

A lot of companies make good boats. Most of them are comparable in construction and quality. The boats are all stable as a rock—both at 60 miles an hour or when drifting—even when there is a 300-pound fisherman on one end and a 150-pound fisherman on the other. The big difference is interior design, what I call the "fishability" of the boat. A bass boat needs lots of storage space. And it needs space on the front and rear decks, where we stand when we fish.

The ride and the handling are the most important things to consider in a boat. When you are on the Mississippi in a winter storm, the waves are five feet high and you are running and gunning and topping and popping, so you want a stable ride and a good-handling boat.

Electronics on the 20-foot boat of a professional angler rival those on some big offshore sport-fishing cruisers.

Your boat and the electronics should not be used as a security blanket. Don't spend all your time working on the boat or playing with your electronics. Use them as a tool and stay focused on the main thing—the bass.

A liquid-crystal depth finder enables the angler to see a picture of the bottom. Stumps and rocks and brush piles are visible. At 240 vertical pixels, the resolution is first-rate.

My global positioning system has a mapping capability that shows me precisely where I am. I was one of the first anglers on the trail to use GPS, and I think it is invaluable as a time-management tool. With fishing spots marked on the GPS, I can go from one to the other without wasting time running and gunning. Since it shows me how far I am from the marina and how long it will take to get there, I can maximize my time on the water during a tournament without running the risk of being fined a pound of fish for every minute I'm late in returning. And in the thickest of fogs or heaviest of rains, I can always find my way back to the marina.

A fisherman must always be able to find his way home.

TIP

~

Don't always accept as gospel what you hear or see from a professional angler.

Just because it works for him doesn't mean it will work for you. Take flipping.

I know professionals who, when they are flipping, set the hook with the line in their hand.

If you do use this method and a big one runs for the boat, what are you going to do?

You are not in control if you set the hook with the line in your hand. And if you are not in control, the fish has the advantage.

Drop the line and set the hook with the rod. That's the purpose of the rod.

Pros don't always do it right.

AN OBSERVATION

~

Generally the very young and the old don't compete well in professional sports. If you are a golfer, you move over to the senior tour or you don't make many checks. Tennis players are over the hill by 35; football, baseball, and basketball players, before that.

But age is not much of a factor in bass fishing. Stan Mitchell was 21 when he won the Classic. Charlie Reed was 51. Stan won in 1981 and Charlie in 1986; both are still fishing the circuit.

This is a sport that calls for a wide variety of technical skills and the ability to exercise at least some control over an infinite number of variables. Yet anyone can do it, from boys who are not yet teenagers to men beyond...well, my dad fished until he died at 84. If it hadn't been for the cancer, he would have fished even longer.

Anyone can enjoy this sport and anyone can be humbled by this sport. In fact, few sports have the potential to humble the professional as much as does bass fishing.

You can take a $30,000 boat, thousands of dollars in electronics, the best charts available, as much local lore as your head can hold, hundreds of choices of high-tech bait and go out on the water and get skunked. You come back to the marina and there, hunkered down on the hill, is an eight-year-old boy with a Snoopy rod and a plastic worm who caught a 20-pound stringer.

I've seen five-year-olds outfish their fathers, and I've seen grandfathers outfish their sons.

Despite the all-American, almost universal appeal of bass fishing, the sport has little respect either in the sporting community or the general population. It does have respect among companies who know this is a 41-billion-dollar business. That's billion with a "B."

Even so, when I tell people I am a professional fisherman, they think I am a commercial fisherman pulling nets on a fishing boat. When my children visit other children and the parents of those children ask, "What does your dad do?" the conversation goes something like this:

"He's a fisherman."

"Well, yes. But what does he do?"

"He fishes."

The parents smile indulgently. "When he goes to work, what does he do?"

"He fishes."

More than 30 million Americans fish for bass. The bass is the number one game fish in America. More money is spent on bass fishing than on golf and tennis combined. Even so, my sport is not regularly reported on in many major newspapers or by news services.

But then I must remember this sport didn't exist until about 30 years ago. Golf has a bit of a head start on us: the first United States Open was in 1895. The forerunner of today's PGA Tour goes back to the early 1920s.

Our time is coming. Television will come to realize the audience potential in a yearly series of 21 tournaments with a payout of more than $6 million. Television will eventually capture the inherent drama of putting 150 fishermen on a lake, cutting their number to 10, and having those men fish for $100,000 when winning is decided by ounces. All this against a backdrop of big water with maybe high winds and thunderstorms thrown in.

It will happen to bass fishing just as it did to golf and to stock car racing. If it weren't for television, stock car racing would be nothing but a bunch of cars running in a circle. Television discovered golf in the late fifties and caused purses to grow almost geometrically. Then television discovered stock car racing. Now it is beginning to sense the potential of bass fishing.

Stock car racing and bass fishing are two of the great subcultures of America. Television and American business discovered and took full advantage of the economic potential in stock car racing.

Now it's our turn.

DOCK TALK

~

In almost every tournament, an angler has to cope with dock talk.

He comes in after ten hours on the water, and maybe he's had a tough day and he hears other anglers talking of all the fish they caught, where they caught them, and how they caught them. So he decides to adjust his game plan.

But what if he is not very strong in the type of fishing the other anglers were talking about?

Dock talk can mislead you and cause you to fish patterns you might not be good at fishing.

Sometimes dock talk is nothing but hearsay.

The pattern you picked and the game plan you are following could be correct. You could catch a sackful the next day by sticking with your plan.

My policy about dock talk is that no matter how good it sounds, I try to ignore it. Partially because I am a loner.

But more so because I believe fishing is like life: You should make your own way.

SOMETHING TO THINK ABOUT

~

In their never-ending search for ways to outwit the bass, anglers sometimes seek out and come to follow what is essentially bad information.

Doug Hannon, "The Bass Professor," uses the behavior of anglers following a tournament to illustrate this point.

As many as 150 professional anglers enter any given tournament. The big question—the focus of virtually every newspaper, magazine, and television story about the winner—focuses on one thing: The lure used by the winner.

Doug believes that when 150 professional anglers go up against each other, the bait that caught the winning number of bass is a fluke—it is not the bait that caught the most bass.

He says that perhaps 80 percent of the bass caught in a given tournament are caught by anglers using the same pattern.

Often the angler who wins does so by doing something off the main pattern—something contrary to the combined skill and judgment of the best bass anglers in the country.

If you want to know what really caught the most fish, Doug

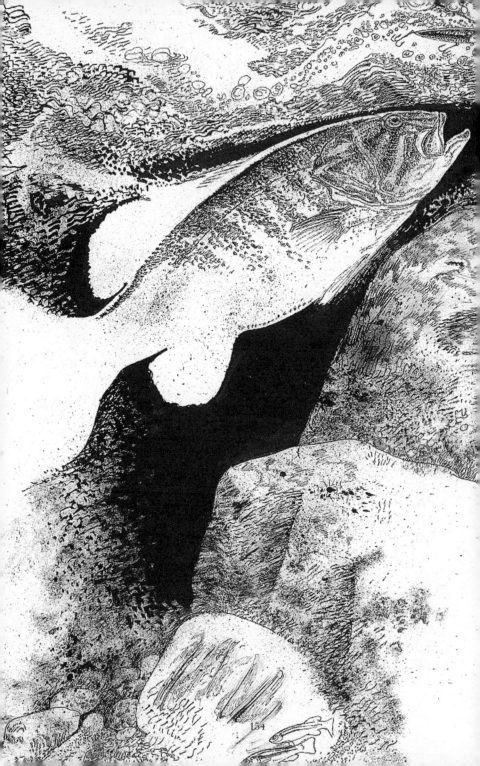

says you should look at the anglers who placed second through tenth. They were on the best pattern.

But there are not enough fish to go around on the best pattern.

Which means that the winner of any given tournament may have won on a fluke.

Anglers should not blindly follow the winner's pattern.

THE THOUSAND ISLANDS

~

One of my favorite places for smallmouth bass is the Thousand Islands in New York. The smallmouth there are extraordinarily aggressive, lightning fast, and the meanest puppies in the water.

I get excited the moment I get on the water up there. I remember one trip when I was throwing a top-water bait on rocks, working the bait fast along the crevasses.

Booooommm!

A smallie hit it.

I set the hook too quickly and missed him. The bait zinged past my shoulder.

I was shaking with excitement when I threw it back.

Kaboooommm!

He hit it again. I saw the water splash and knew that this time I had him.

I set the hook.

Again I was too fast and missed him, and the bait came out of the water at about a hundred miles an hour. It was a blur when it shot past me four feet above the water.

I looked down and there in the clear water I saw the bass tracking the bait. Unbelievable!

The bait was at mach speed over the water, and the fish was

staying underneath it, tracking it. Man, my adrenaline was really pumping.

The bait hit the water and he gobbled it.

He had the bait and I had about 30 feet of slack line. As he swam away, I was reeling in ten-foot sections of line, trying to set the hook.

He blew the bait.

The smallie won.

But I had the experience of a lifetime.

FISHING CLOSE

~

Here's a tip that has enabled me to make a check in many tournaments.

Waters around the launch site or around the marina usually have good fish. Fishing in these waters is called fishing close. It is a long-favored tournament tactic.

My variation on this tactic is that I don't use it until the last day of practice. I want to let the other anglers get in there first and beat it up. If I catch fish there after other anglers have been there, then I know I can rely on that spot during the tournament.

But if I fish it the first day, other anglers could come in later and beat it up. And then if I need it and am depending on it, I've made a bad tactical decision.

And I won't make a check.

So fish close.

But fish late.

TAPE RECORDERS

~

Penny Berryman, a well-known female angler, had a tournament coming up in the Lake George area of the St. Johns River and asked me to show her the water. Every time I pointed out a bass habitat or a good place to fish, she dictated notes into a small tape recorder.

I thought using a tape recorder was an interesting practice. I also thought that I didn't have time to stop and dictate while I was fishing.

Later I was fishing a tournament in Lake Okeechobee. During practice I pulled into a little ditch loaded with one- and two-pounders. I didn't fish there long because I needed bigger fish. I thought the ditch had possibilities, and if I needed the little fish then I'd come back.

I did well in the tournament. But on the last day, thunderstorms came up and the wind and rain lashed the lake. I couldn't catch big fish. I sat there wondering where I should go and what I should do. I still had several hours before weigh-in. But I bombed. I went from being in the top 10 down to about 30.

It was not until I was driving home that I remembered the ditch filled with one- and two-pounders, with fish that would have kept me in the top ten.

I also remembered the tape recorder. And suddenly I saw its value.

I began using a tape recorder when fishing new water.

Before I'd go to sleep, I'd lay the tape recorder on my chest, hit the Play button, and listen to my notes from that day.

The notes burned into my brain. The details remained fresh.

"I got a strike on that rocky point when the wind was blowing on it."

"I caught one here."

"I lost one there."

I listened to my notes and visually relived the entire day. And then in the heat of the tournament, I remembered the spots.

Many times I've listened to a tape and discovered a pattern that I hadn't noticed when I was on the water.

The recorder is particularly valuable during spawning season, when I might find bass in 50 locations on a lake. It is impossible to remember all of them. If I get to the last day and need a five-pounder to win—and I can't remember the locations—I've lost an opportunity.

Now with the tape recorder, I remember and run there to catch him.

It happened in a Megabucks Tournament on the Harris chain of lakes at Leesburg, Florida. I remembered, with the help of my recorder, a seven-pounder I had seen in a canal. I went through the locks and ran down to the spot, shut down, dropped the trolling motor, and almost immediately saw a three-pounder. I turned and there was the seven-pounder.

A tape recorder can be very important to an angler.

THE BASS

~

Bass in some lakes are smarter than bass in other lakes.

Fish in Florida lakes are the smartest of all. They have been fished a lot and are far more cautious. They've been there, done that, and swam away with the T-shirt. They are hard to catch.

When an angler who has fished Florida lakes goes up north, he finds a strange phenomenon: Anglers there have historically fished for walleye, muskie, or northern pike. They think bass are a trash fish and a nuisance. As a result, northern bass often are ridiculously easy to catch.

Northern bass haven't had the pressure. They are not yet programmed.

But that is changing. We are now having tournaments—big tournaments—with more than 300 anglers on Thousand Islands, Lake Champlain, Lake St. Clair, Lake Minnetonka, and a dozen other northern lakes and rivers.

Northern bass are getting smarter.

AID AND ASSISTANCE

~

Top fishermen are like top contenders in any other professional sport: They search out every possible avenue that might lead them to a championship.

Dion Hibdon won the Classic in 1997. Everyone thinks it is because of his skill in skipping baits up under docks. But it was not because of a special bait or a highly skilled technique. It was because he changed his thinking.

He won the mental game.

Dion is a great fisherman. If he enters a tournament, he usually gets a check.

But he was always near the top, never at the top. He was catching plenty of fish, but a lot of them were breaking off. He was getting the bites but not getting the fish. And it began to affect his thinking.

Before the Classic he went to a sports psychologist. He came out of those sessions not worrying about the ones that got away, but believing that for every one that got away, another fish was waiting to be caught.

Four bass broke off his line the final day of the Classic, and he missed another 20 strikes. But he believed the bass would bite. He then caught his biggest fish and won the Classic.

At some point in the pursuit of the bass, we absorb just about all the science, all the technique, and all the skills we can contain.

Then we have to move into the mind.

It is in the mind that we find the ability to catch and keep the big ones.

PASSION

~

One year I had five tournaments back-to-back—five weeks on the road going from one lake to another. Then a two-day break and three more tournaments. It was a grueling two months on the road.

When I got home in Gainesville, I pulled my flats boat over to the Gulf of Mexico and went fly fishing for tarpon.

More than 90 percent of the anglers on the tournament trail spend their off days doing anything other than fishing. They relax by hunting, playing golf, watching television, working in the yard, or simply resting.

I relax by going fishing.

Fishing is my passion. My love for this sport grows every year. Except for my religion and my family, fishing is the most important thing in my life—my vocation and my avocation, my work and my play. I've fished since I was a child. And yet every time I see a fish, I grow weak in the knees. My body trembles and my voice rises.

I still get pumped up.

I love every minute I am on the water.

It's just too bad there is no Olympic category for professional bass fishing.

I'd take a shot at it.

"I was fishing the Classic on Logan Martin.
It was the last day and I was struggling.
I had broken my line three times.
I had a good tournament and now
it was down to the last two or three hours,
and I was trying to make this thing happen
too fast. I was losing it. Shaw pulled up on me
and said, 'Hang in there, Dion. You got plenty
of daylight left.' He talked to me for a while
and settled me back down. I fished good after
that. I caught my best three fish
after Shaw talked to me. I won the Classic.
At weigh-in, when they announced I was
the winner, I thanked Shaw.
Everybody likes Shaw.
He's a straight shooter."

—Dion Hibdon

WOMEN AND CHILDREN

~

I have talked often of fathers and sons being on the water. But fishing should not be confined to fathers and sons; it should be parents and children. Women, especially single moms, should become more involved in bass fishing and less reluctant to take their children—boys or girls—to a lake or river.

Few things are as deeply rooted in the America psyche as the ritual of the family going down to the pond or to the creek bank to have a picnic and go fishing. Family is the operative word here. Look out on the lakes and rivers of America, and you will see boats filled with families.

If a family is a mom and a child, that family, too, can picnic and fish.

For the woman who knows little about fishing and who doesn't know how to begin selecting tackle and baits, B.A.S.S. is a good place to start. The CastingKids program is run through the 2,700 local fishing clubs all around America. It teaches kids the basics: flipping, pitching, casting, and bait selection.

The B.A.S.S. Fishing Techniques Institute sends professional anglers around the country to teach weekend classes on just about anything that anyone needs to know about bass fishing. And there are many colleges and universities that teach continuing-education courses on bass fishing.

At my seminars around the country, I look out into the audience and see lots of women who fish and who want to learn more, who want to teach their children.

We must find new and creative ways to bring more women into our sport. B.A.S.S. and every other professional group as well as every angler, amateur, and professional should become more involved in finding ways for women to learn about fishing, to take part in fishing, and to get their children involved in fishing.

Fishing is one of the oldest, strongest, and brightest threads in the tapestry of American life.

It must remain that way.

THE RECORD

~

The largemouth bass can grow to be an enormous fish.

The world record of 22 pounds 4 ounces was set on June 2, 1932. The fish was caught in Montgomery Lake by a 20-year-old farmer named George Perry. Montgomery Lake is in southeast Georgia near the tiny town of Helena. It is an old oxbow lake of maybe an acre, very shallow, and it gets new water only when the Ocmulgee River floods.

George Perry used an old homemade boat, made from $1.25 worth of plywood, to get out on the lake. His bait-casting reel and tackle was worth less than $10. He used a wooden broken-back Creek Chub Wiggle Fish lure that had glass eyes, hand-painted gills, and a metal tail that flapped. It cost $1.25.

Times were hard in Georgia in 1932, and young George Perry supported his mother, two younger brothers, and a sister. His family ate the big bass. It took them three days.

George Perry's record has stood for almost seven decades. It is the longest standing record for any major freshwater fish in America. Despite the incredible advances in technology, boats, rods, reels, and electronics, and all that we have since learned about the bass, the record stands.

Today the biggest bass in the world are believed to be in Florida. In fact, the Florida largemouth—*Micropterus salmoides floridanus*—is recognized as a subspecies of the black bass. The Florida largemouth has been shipped to nurseries, lakes, and rivers all over the country to grow and prosper—and to show other states what real bass fishing can be like. It has been imported in large numbers to Texas and California. Both states have innovative breeding programs to improve the strain even further.

Florida is my home state. But I disagree with those who say that when the world record is broken, it will be by a fish caught in Florida. Our lakes are shallow and our climate has heated them beyond their historical temperatures. A bass needs a more moderate climate and plenty of food to grow bigger than 22 pounds.

I think the new world record will come from California or Texas. And I believe it could happen in the next five years.

PETA AND OTHERS

~

Pete Thliveros and I were fishing Lake George when we saw a big bass on top of the water. She was sluggish and lethargic. I put a net under her and scooped her out of the water. She had a bluegill lodged in her mouth. Bass eat fish head first, so the bluegill's sharp dorsal fin and its gills prevented the bass from spitting it out. The bluegill was beginning to putrefy and the bass was dying.

She weighed in at ten pounds four ounces.

Peter T. took the bluegill out of her mouth, got rid of the spines stuck in her throat, then put her in an aerated tank and fed and nursed her back to health. Afterward he released her back into her home territory. I have no doubt, none whatsoever, that if she saw another bluegill, she would try to eat it. If she felt any pain from the spines, she'd quickly forget it.

It reminded me of the years when we tagged fish before we released them. I can't tell you how many fish I caught that were tagged. Some fish were caught over and over. So the trauma of being hooked, if there is a trauma, is obviously quickly forgotten. The released bass goes out there and continues to eat artificial lures.

Doug Hannon, who knows more about bass than most people, says the average young bass has been caught 1½ times, which means that by the time he reaches four, five, or six pounds, he has been caught more times than he can remember.

That's why I don't understand PETA and some of the movie stars who support PETA. Those people say bass have feeling in their mouths and that snagging one will traumatize it for life. They say bass fishing is cruel to fish.

I've talked to several fisheries experts about this. Dr. Bob Reinert at the University of Georgia says that because our mouths are filled with nerve endings and are very sensitive, we have a tendency to think it is the same with all animals. But it's not. He also says that the part of the brain having to do with the pain center is almost nonexistent in fish.

"We work in the lab with fish," he said. "We implant transmitters in them and they swim off. They don't perceive pain the way we do."

He says there are ponds where fish are caught seven or eight times; and that while they feel pressure when they are hooked and an angler is reeling them in, they do not feel pain.

Any fisheries biologist will tell you that bass eat crawfish and bluegills. Their favorite foods have things that cause the food to stick, bite, or pinch.

Bass anglers are some of the most ardent conservationists in America. We know how fragile this sport is, and we want it to be there for our children and our grandchildren. We are not going to do anything to jeopardize the sport for us or our legacy.

Our environmental and conservation record goes back 30 years and will stand four-square with that of any environmental group in America. Our record is based on solid scientific principle. We have led some of the most important environmental battles in America.

And for those who say conservation and fishing are mutually exclusive, that one cannot be an ardent sportsman and a strong conservationist. I say that Teddy Roosevelt did a pretty good job of doing both.

And so have millions of bass anglers.

A TALE OF TWO MEN
~

In 1986, Charlie Reed won the Classic on Chickamauga Lake near Chattanooga. The next year George Cochran won on the Ohio River in Kentucky.

Charlie does not like going to fishing or product shows, conducting seminars, or making speeches. He doesn't like to be away from home and family. He wants to fish and be with his family. He took his prize money and turned down almost all the chances for more money from promotional opportunities. He kept on fishing.

George is another story. When he won the Classic, he quit his job as a railroad brakeman and devoted himself to full-time promotional work. His fee for making a speech jumped from $300 to $1,000. He was on the road almost 300 days that year. He would come in from a week on the road, and his wife—who quit her job to be his full-time secretary-manager—would hand him a freshly packed suitcase. He'd be gone for another week. He'd begin tournaments without practicing. But he knew his time had come and that he had to take advantage of it.

George used his Classic winnings to send his children to college and to put aside money for retirement.

Charlie took his prize money and kept his family and his fishing as the focus of his life.

George made as much money off the Classic as anyone ever has.

Charlie just loved to fish.

You can make of this sport anything you want.

Mounting Fish

~

Back in the fifties and sixties and into the early seventies, anytime an angler caught a big bass, he had it mounted and hung on his wall. Many fishing guides who wanted to boost their business, and their egos, also had their fish mounted. There must be millions of these mounted fish in homes and offices all across America.

This is the great shame of bass fishing.

But back then we didn't know any better.

We do know better today, and it is time for this practice to end.

The fish that anglers have mounted are almost always females.

And any angler who kills a female to have her mounted has prevented that fish from spawning again. He also has taken out of the system the DNA that made her so large.

It's not important that she might be the angler's first big bass.

It's not important that she might be the biggest bass the angler ever caught.

What is important is that it took her years to become such a big fish. She survived more trials and tribulations than most of us can imagine. When she was a fry, she avoided becoming a meal for male bass. When she was a fingerling, she continued to avoid predatory fish and predatory wading birds. When she became a young bass, she avoided being eaten by ospreys and eagles, or otters or alligators. As she grew even larger, she survived countless attempts by fishermen to catch her. She survived drought and flood and agricultural run-off, pollution and disease.

She survived the modern day equivalent of biblical plagues.

She deserves to live and to pass on the qualities that enabled her to survive.

She does not deserve the indignity of being killed and placed on a wall so an angler can show her off to visitors.

A mounted bass does not reveal prowess as an angler. A mounted bass reveals the angler is selfish. It reveals that the angler has forever affected the genetics of bass in the body of water where she was caught. Big bass are rare and cannot be replaced. Their genes are gone. Subsequent fish spawned from other females will be smaller.

If anglers want to remember their large bass and to show their concern for this sport, here is what they should do.

Be prepared for the day when the big one bites. Put a tape measure, a small set of scales, and a disposable camera in the boat. When the big one is caught, take plenty of pictures. Measure the length and girth of the fish. Weigh her.

Then release her.

Take the photographs and the measurements to a shop and have them do a fiberglass mount of the fish. It looks better than a skin mount; in fact, an observer has to get in very close and study the fine details to detect that it is not a skin mount.

A fiberglass mount does not look ratty a decade later.

Another option is to take a photo of the bass, blow up the picture as big as you want, then have it framed along with the bait that caught the fish. I've done this.

No angler should kill a big bass.

Guides should not allow their clients to keep a big bass.

Every big bass should be released.

ARMS AND BACKS

~

Most sports call for occasional peaks of mental intensity, times when the athlete must exert maximum concentration. In golf, for instance, it is when the golfer is hitting the ball, and in tennis, the intensity lasts for the length of a volley.

But an angler must always be ready, always at his peak intensity. In a tournament, every cast could bring a strike worth $100,000. In addition to always expecting a strike, the angler is constantly planning his next cast and searching for productive water.

Long hours and long days of such intensity can cause mental strain. Physically, it's even worse.

The first things to go on a professional angler are his arms and back.

His arms, because when he is on the water he is casting about four times a minute. Maybe more. In a day on the water, he throws out the bait at least 1,500 times. In three days of practice and a three-day tournament, that's 9,000 casts.

Bass elbow is the same as tennis elbow. But it seems more severe because the onslaught is so rapid.

An angler's back goes because when a shallow-draft bass boat is running and gunning he takes a real pounding. If winds and waves are high and the angler is topping and popping, being on the water is brutal.

Some anglers wear back braces when they are on the water.

If you consider the days of practice fishing and the three-day tournaments—sometimes done in extreme weather—and that in the fall and spring these tournaments are often back-to-back, it is easy to see why we must be in good physical condition.

For years I have worked out with weights. I carry a five-pound barbell when I am on the road. At night, after a day on the water, I sit down, stretch out my arms, and do full rotations to support and build my wrists and arms. I also do stretching exercises.

The better shape an angler is in, the better he will do on the water.

And the longer he will last.

SCHEDULE

~

My schedule was such that when I went to Lake Sam Rayburn to fish a tournament, I had to leave Gainesville a week in advance.

Thursday morning I left home very early for a nine-hour drive to Baton Rouge, where I parked my van and boat. Friday morning I was up at 5:30 a.m. for a flight to Chicago, where I worked a boat show all day. I had dinner and then checked into my hotel about 10 p.m. Saturday I was up at 4:30 for the 30-minute taxi ride to the airport and a flight to St. Louis, where I worked an in-store promotion. I got to bed about 11.

The next morning there was an early flight back to Baton Rouge for a day off.

Monday morning I flew to Louisville and worked a boat and travel show, did a seminar, and got to bed about 11. Tuesday morning I flew to Kansas City for two days to work the boat show. It was almost ten each evening before I got to a restaurant for dinner and close to midnight before I got to bed.

An early morning flight Thursday to Baton Rouge and a four-hour drive got me to Rayburn, where I practice-fished Friday. On Saturday I drove to Beaumont for an in-store promotion. Then I drove back to the lake and practice-fished another three days before fishing the tournament.

From Rayburn it was a 14-hour drive to Nashville, where I had to pick up a new boat. I was there a half-day, then drove five hours to Atlanta for two days' work. The next afternoon I drove five hours back home to Gainesville.

This was a normal road trip.

I spend a lot of time on my car phone while I'm traveling. Polly handles my tournament scheduling, travel details, and coordinates everything with my sponsors. She and I talk every day when I'm on the road.

I put about 50,000 miles a year on my van and another 50,000 on airplanes. My gas, hotels, meals, and entry fees cost about $40,000 annually. I stay in such a state of intense concentration that when I come home after a road trip, I have several of what Polly calls "broccoli days." I sit in my chair like a lump of broccoli and do nothing. Polly knows that this is not the time to present me with what she calls a "Honey do" list—as in "Honey do this" or "Honey do that." She does much of what needs to be done around the house.

There are some things about this lifestyle I do not like. I was not at home to comfort Amy when her cat died. I missed my son's birthday one year.

Sometimes I pull out a copy of a letter that dad wrote to his father-in-law in Germany back in 1991. He said, "I am very proud that my son is ranked as the tenth-best bass fisherman in the world. I'm very glad that I did not have the opportunity to be a professional bass fisherman. It's a hard life, and he is missing the most beautiful part of his life with his son and daughter."

I read the letter again after I returned home from a long road trip. I was sitting in my chair talking with Shaw-Shaw when I saw that he was tinkering with a tackle box filled with baits. Then he began tying a fly. And I realized he was like my dad and me in so many ways.

The circle remains unbroken.

JAPAN

~

One of the most amazing things about bass fishing is how this sport, which originated among the good old boys of the rural

South, has leaped oceans to become a popular sport in so many countries around the world.

Bass fishing is particularly big in Japan.

Top Japanese anglers are good enough to win B.A.S.S. tournaments and to qualify for the Classic.

Norio Tanabe became the first Japanese angler to win a B.A.S.S. tournament. It was on Kentucky Lake in 1993.

Takahiro Omori won a B.A.S.S. tournament on Lake of the Ozarks in 1996. He is very popular. I've fished with him; he's a great guy.

In 1997, Toshinari Namiki became the first Japanese angler to qualify for the Classic. He was followed around by more TV crews and reporters, all from Japan, than I have ever seen follow an angler. He is only 31. He and his wife, Yuki, travel all around America fishing the tournaments.

The biggest outdoor show on Japanese television is a bass fishing show produced by Ken Suzuki, the owner of a chain of outdoor stores.

I've conducted fishing seminars in Japan. Most bass in Japan are in the two- to four-pound range, but there are lakes where six- or seven-pounders are found.

What is even more astonishing than the growth of bass fishing in Japan is the Japanese influence on bass fishing in America.

The next time you go to a competition, look at the tournament shirts worn by professional anglers. You'll be surprised at how many logos you see from Japanese sponsors.

The Japanese make a full range of fishing products that are used by American anglers.

When bass fishing first started in Japan, the lures were all handmade. Some of them cost around $200 and were kept in locked cabinets in the tackle stores.

Today Japanese baits are not that expensive, but they are still more expensive than most American baits. They are in the $10 to $30 range and are some of the most technologically advanced on the market. In one Japanese jerk bait, there is an inside chamber that contains small weights. When you cast, centrifugal force throws the weights to the rear of the lure and you can sling the bait like a bullet. Then when it hits the water, the weights roll forward in the chamber and cause the bait to sit level. It is a great bait.

Because a bait is expensive doesn't mean the bass will take it. A bass doesn't look out from under a lily pad and say, "Wow! That's a $30 bait. I'm going to bite that one."

But I think it is amazing that the Japanese have applied so much technology to advance a sport that began in America's rural South.

SWIMMING POOLS

~

Before I enter a big tournament such as the Classic, I test every bait that I will use. I sharpen all the hooks or put on new hooks, then test it in the swimming pool at my house.

A bait can look good when you hold it but perform erratically in the water.

You might have a mental picture of how it performs, when in fact it performs another way.

I want to look in the clear water of a swimming pool and see how it bounces off the bottom. Does it collapse and do nothing? Does it dig? Does it wiggle? How does it look when it hesitates?

If you know how a bait works underwater, you can visualize what it is doing once you begin fishing a tournament.

I cast each bait three or four times in the pool. Then I tune it and cast it again.

Afterwards I mark each bait under the throat so that when I pick it out of the tackle box during a tournament, I can see at a glance what sort of bait I have. A single check means a good bait; a check and a plus mean an excellent bait; a check and a plus-plus is a bait that will reach out and grab them.

Finally I wash the baits thoroughly to get rid of the chlorine from the pool.

Preparation is the key.

LUCK

~

Larry Lazoen was fishing a spinner bait on an underwater point in Lake Murray, South Carolina. The point was covered with weeds and grass, but there was a big bald spot on top. Visibility was about two feet in the stained water.

Larry was reeling in his bait to the tip of his rod when suddenly the head of a seven-pounder appeared. Larry knew if he pulled back the rod to cast, the bass would disappear. Instinctively he jabbed the rod toward the bass. The fish gobbled the bait off the tip of his rod.

A lot of people said he was the luckiest angler on the water that day.

Fishing and luck are words that seem to go together.

Everyone talks about luck. You're easing out of the marina about daylight and someone on the dock wishes you good luck. Or you're on the dock at sundown as anglers are returning from a day on the water and you hear one of them say, "I caught a limit today. I got lucky."

I know one angler who has a pair of good-luck shorts that he wears when he fishes the Classic. Others follow little rituals when they're on the water to bring good luck.

I've even heard anglers say, "I'd rather be lucky than good."

Not me. I'll take good anytime.

Good is forever.

Luck, or whatever it is that people call luck, is here and there and gone.

Too many anglers have the idea that luck is a big part of fishing. I don't believe in luck.

I believe that opportunity and preparation sometime meet, and that meeting place is thought by some to be luck.

Larry caught his seven-pounder not because he was lucky, but because when opportunity and preparation met, he was ready.

If an angler is on the water and has the opportunity to catch a big one, and he is prepared when the big one strikes, and he catches the fish, is that luck?

I go on the water with a head full of options. I know what I will do if the water is up, and I know what I will do if the water is down. I know what I will do if the water is clear or if the water is muddy. I know where the fish should be holding, and I know what baits to throw.

Where is luck involved?

THE TOURNAMENT

~

Professional anglers like to tell the story about the tournament on Lake Lanier, north of Atlanta. A local bartender who heard that 300 fishermen were arriving stocked up his bar and brought in additional servers. But on the first night of the tournament, his sales remained flat. Not a single hard-drinking fishermen did he see.

The next afternoon the bartender stopped one of the fishermen and said, "Why don't you guys like my bar?"

"We don't like any bar," he was told.

I've heard an angler say, "I can't fish a hangover pattern. And staring at the sun strobing off the water when I have a hangover is not my idea of fun."

Even though bass anglers stay sober, the hotels and motels where they stay during a tournament are too noisy and too busy for me. There are too many boats and vehicles for the available parking spaces. So I rarely stay in the hotel with most of the other anglers. Instead I get a room in a nearby hotel where there might be only a few other contestants.

In my early days on the trail, I roomed with one or two friends. But now I use the evenings to prepare my equipment and to work on my mental game, then I go to bed around 8:30. The tournament stakes are too high for me to toss and turn and not be able to sleep because my roommate wants to stay up late and watch TV.

The night before a tournament begins, I fill the gas tanks on the boat and make sure the oil is topped off.

Bass fishermen usually ask for a room that is "down and out"— downstairs and on the outside. And we always try to park our boats in front of our rooms so we can keep an eye on them. I run a flat extension cord from an outlet in my room to the battery chargers on the boat. A flat extension cord is necessary because a round one will not fit under the door.

I eat dinner about 5:30 or 6 and then go to my room. I use a line stripper and pull the line from the eight or ten reels I'll be using in competition. I replace it with new line. I carefully tie new knots and check and double-check to make sure they are hard and true.

I go over my game plan and my tactics and pull out the appropriate baits. I check those baits again to make sure they are in good condition. I pay particular attention to the hooks, making sure they're sharp.

Everything that I can control, I do. Because there are so many things that cannot be controlled.

I need to be up early, sometimes 3:30 or 4 a.m. You'd be surprised how many motels ignore you when you ask for a 3:30 a.m. wake-up call. So I have two alarm clocks, plus an alarm on my wristwatch.

I can't afford to oversleep when I'm fishing for $100,000.

When the alarm goes off, I head for the shower, turning on the weather channel as I pass the TV set. I want a last-minute forecast so I can dress appropriately. When I come out of the shower, I apply 30 SPF sunscreen.

If it is cold and rainy, I put on warm clothes and a rain suit before I leave the room. Then I go out and unplug the chargers, take the cover off the boat, and tie down my rods and reels. I go to the ice machine and fill up the cooler in my boat.

Rarely is there time for breakfast, so I eat a sandwich while driving to the marina.

I want to be one of the first four or five guys on the water. It allows me to settle down, go over my game plan, and get mentally prepared. I don't want to be rushed.

If the weather is cold, I want to be out on the water early to let my body get acclimated to the cold.

If it is going to be a hot day, I double-check the aerated live wells and my supply of ice. Lake water at 90° does not contain as much oxygen as lake water at 60°. So when I catch fish, I will put a generous amount of ice into the live well. Then, rather than pumping in fresh lake water, I recirculate the water in the live well. I check to make sure I have plenty of a commercial preparation to replenish the slime coating on the fish.

I tie the boat to a slip, then sit in the boat rechecking my baits and knots. I hook up my electronics.

I wash my hands in a fish scent.

I prepare my mind.

In a few moments the marina is bedlam. There may be 150 boats being launched, and trucks and vans are pouring in. They back down the ramp quickly, almost all of them getting it right the first time. They release their boats to drift across the marina, then hitch a ride out to the boat with another angler.

If there is fog over the water, the start will be delayed. But we are all ready to take off at safe light. An hour before take-off, the marina is filled with more than a hundred boats. White lights shine from poles on the sterns; red and green lights gleam on the bows. I watch friends in other boats nod and say, "Go catch 'em."

Then it's time to go.

The pros on the B.A.S.S. circuit know how to operate their boats. They generally are quick and smooth—they're professionals—and rarely are there problems. But in some of the other tournaments, the anglers are not as skilled and occasionally shouts to avoid collisions are heard.

Boats are released in flights. The anglers know that they are in the first, second, third, or whatever flight, and accordingly move closer to the starting line. The tournament director is there with a bullhorn. As he calls our names, we idle by his position for a final boat check of the kill switch, life jackets, and operating live well. Then he launches the first flight, and we push the throttles forward, drilling holes in the water.

After the first 20 or 30 boats have taken off, the water at the starting point looks as if the perfect storm had formed. If I am in a later flight, I punch through the confused water, bouncing, prop cavitating, spray flying, then I'm up on plane, running flat out, pulling only inches of water. There is a long string of boats across the water by then.

We scatter into the dawn while most people are still asleep. We are looking for waters where the bass is hiding. There are almost no wakes from these boats once they are up and running. A slight wash from the engine's lower unit is the only sign of our passage—that and a big rooster tail of spray and the growl of a 200hp engine that tears apart the dawn and tells people for a mile in every direction that more than a hundred fishermen are scorching the waters, looking for the bass.

At these tournaments, especially toward the end of a season, I look around and see the best bass anglers in the world. These men have survived and done well during another year on the trail. If the fish are out there, they will find them.

If we don't find fish, we have to find another line of work.

If I am fortunate enough to draw a low number and be in the first flight, I'm running for my primary spot. If I have a high number and launch in the last flight, I go there and hope no one else has also found the spot. But sometimes they have. So then I'm off again, running for another spot.

I drop my trolling motor and make the first cast of the day.

And each time I realize all over again how lucky I am to do what I do—to know the magic of the water, to live my dream.

That's all.

And that's enough.

THE CLASSIC

~

The Classic is the single most important tournament in the life of a professional angler. The winning angler is considered the world-champion bass fisherman. That means sponsors come flocking to your door. It means you suddenly have enough prestige to last a lifetime. Being decreed the best bass fisherman in the world means a million dollars in earnings and prize money.

Winning the Classic means your life is changed forever.

Being second means nothing.

I know.

I have finished second.

You don't fish the Classic to place. You fish to win.

That means your tactics are different. In other tournaments you try to catch a limit and then go after the kicker. In the Classic you go after the most fish and the biggest fish.

You have to take chances.

Big chances.

You have to put your career and everything you think you know about bass on the line.

You have to fish patterns that might not be productive for most of the time. But you fish them, knowing that when the pattern starts working—if it starts working—you might get the big bites that will make you the winner.

You go head to head with Mr. Bass. Head to head against a ticking clock. You go for broke knowing if your pattern does not hold, you will suffer the embarrassment of standing in front of 25,000 spectators with no fish. You go for broke knowing that a month after the Classic, the television broadcast of the tournament will be aired and your humiliation will be forever.

That's why you sometimes see the best bass anglers in the world—tired, sunburned, and bedraggled—bringing to weigh-in one or two fish barely over the minimum allowable size. Their pattern did not hold, and at the end of the day they had to scratch, work hard to catch something, anything, in order to save face.

That's why you sometimes see great anglers come to weigh-in with an empty bag.

And on their faces and in their voices is the restrained frustration of knowing they picked the wrong pattern; that if had they had fished another pattern, they might be standing there with a bag of bass big enough to make them the new world champion.

The Classic is winner take all.

AUTOGRAPHS

~

I know of no other sport where top professionals are as available to fans as they are in tournament bass fishing.

If you're a NASCAR fan and want an autograph from Jeff Gordon, forget it. Trying to get a minute of Michael Jordan's time just won't happen. You can't just walk up to Tiger Woods and get an autograph. And there are some baseball players who, if they sign autographs, want to be paid for doing so.

But bass anglers remain a bunch of guys available and accessible to the fans. At the Classic, a full day is set aside for contenders to meet fans, sign autographs, and talk fishing. We know that this is the part of our sport that makes us unique.

Professional anglers almost always carry laundry marking pens so they can autograph shirts and hats.

Upwards of 20,000 fans attend the Classic on the final day, and most of them spend hours at the accompanying outdoor show. After weigh-in, I always go to the outdoor show to sign autographs.

A line forms immediately when I begin signing autographs. It is a personal policy of mine never to simply stand up and walk out while there are still people who want autographs. It doesn't matter what might be happening elsewhere, I will sign autographs for every person in line. But timing is critical because there is a black-tie reception and dinner in the evening.

As the time approaches for the reception, I walk toward the exit while still signing autographs for the last dozen or so people in line. If I don't finish by the time I reach the door, the last two or three people come outside with me. Usually there are a couple of minutes of spare time for us to chat.

Twenty minutes before the reception begins, I dash to my room to change into a dinner jacket.

And I am happy because I know that anyone who wanted my autograph got it. Most bass anglers feel the same way.

TELEVISION

~

Millions of people watch bass fishing shows on television.

If you are a viewer, you should know that TV fishing is first of all a business, a business that must attract viewers. Producers of most television shows think that when the camera is on a fisherman, he has to catch a lot of fish. Big fish. The show has to be exciting. That makes sense. Why have a fishing show if the host is not catching fish?

But some TV shows where the host slam-dunks the bass every time he goes on the water are ego-driven shows. It's as if the host is saying, "I am a great fisherman, and I will show you how to catch a ton of fish."

These shows also do a terrible injustice to viewers. Fishermen get the idea that every time they go fishing, they're supposed to catch monster fish. A lot of them.

But some days you don't catch monster fish. Some days you don't catch any fish. What you catch most of the time are five bass weighing a total of six pounds. That's what real fishing is for most fishermen.

Then you remember the TV show and feel inferior, and you say to yourself, "This is not the sport for me. I think I'll go play golf or tennis."

Part of the problem is the network. They used to say, "We have to have big fish. We don't want to see any little fish. We want three-pounders and up."

What we need are more fishing shows that demonstrate true fishing. I try to make my show true. If I catch only little ones, I show the little ones.

I was taping a show on Lake Guntersville in Alabama, and the biggest fish I caught was a two-pounder. I showed it on the air.

On my show we don't fudge and we don't change the fish. We don't use tank fish.

What I get is what you see.

This might sound self-serving. But watch the show and decide for yourself.

I've been doing this long enough that usually I can go out there and catch fish. But there are still days when I get zeroed.

By watching a fishing show, you can tell if the host is only a host or if he is a true fisherman.

THE SPORT

~

I know a five-year-old boy who caught a limit of bass on a bait-casting reel.

Can you imagine a five-year-old breaking 70 in golf or playing tennis at Wimbledon?

I come back to this thing about age and bass fishing because it is so important. It is the essence of being a bass angler.

I don't know of another sport that not only appeals to such a wide variety of ages, but that can be done well by both the very young and the old.

It is important that sons be taken fishing by their fathers. Not just because fishing and childhood are inextricably tied together, and not just because of the lasting memories that arise when a boy fishes with his father. If a boy is taken fishing, he probably will remain an angler as a man.

I don't know any professional bass anglers who went fishing for the first time as adults.

They began as youngsters, just as I did with my dad.

Those of us who have fished since childhood are the luckiest people on earth. The things that our fathers taught us, we teach our sons.

The appeal to all ages is what makes bass fishing such a phenomenon.

We are all equal on the water.

HONEY HOLES

~

During the practice fishing of a lake before a tournament, a friend found a creek that was blocked by blowdowns. The fallen trees prevented boats from proceeding up the creek. Or so most of the anglers thought.

When my friend came in that night, he put a chain saw in his boat and covered it with a towel so no one could see it. The next day he waited until late in the afternoon, when almost everyone was off the water, and pulled out his chain saw, cut through the log jam, and moved on up the creek.

He caught a ton of fish in there.

He found a honey hole.

One of my favorite patterns during practice days before a tournament is to go up a creek as far as my boat will go, then get out and wade around until I find a small channel I can push the boat through. I'm looking for a channel big enough that, once the tournament starts, I can navigate beyond the point that everyone thinks marks the end of navigable waters. Beyond the shallow water and the last sandbar and what looks to be silted-in waters, I often find good water that rarely if ever has been fished before. I catch a lot of fish in such water.

Every angler looks for a honey hole.

We all dream of that place where we can catch a fish on every cast, that place where every time we hook a fish, another 20 fish rise to the surface.

Maybe once in a lifetime we find a great honey hole in a lake. But in big water, the honey hole never lasts for long. The bass is migratory. Bass also feel the pressure. Catch a lot of them, and they quickly move to another location.

At a tournament in Florida, Gary Klein caught eight fish on nine casts—four- and five-pounders. After weigh-in, my kids and I got in the boat with Gary; he took us there and lined us up on the spot.

Every time I hooked a fish, I handed the rod to Amy; and every time Gary hooked a fish, he handed the rod to Shaw-Shaw. My son caught an 11-pounder. If Gary had caught that fish during the tournament, he would have won a boat, motor, and trailer.

We told another friend about the honey hole. But when he arrived, the fish had moved on.

All across America are remote creeks filled with bass. Too often the angler stops when he comes to a blowdown across the creek, when the banks narrow and he can't turn the boat around, or when he sees the water ahead is silted-in or filled with stumps.

I don't carry a chain saw, but I often carry a handsaw in my boat. You can, too. Or tie your boat to the blowdown, grab your tackle, walk around the blowdown, and go farther up the creek. All you need is a piece of water big enough to let your bait start working. It might be a pool no more than two or three feet across. And there is always another pool beyond that.

Find yourself a honey hole.

DIALING IN

~

Don't take baggage on the water.

Approach the bass with your mind clear. Focus on the fish and on fishing. Allow the bass to lead you in the right direction.

Trust your instincts. Trust that little voice in the back of your head. There is always a voice saying consider this or do this.

Listen.

Listen and heed.

So many times when I've been on the water a little voice has made all the difference.

I'd be racing up a lake and hear, *Fish right here* or *Fish that bank.*

I caught fish every time. It was not luck and it was not coincidence. I knew exactly where I should fish, and I knew ahead of time I would get bit.

I was dialed in.

You won't hear many anglers talk about this publicly, but at the upper levels of competition, bass fishing enters the realm of the mystical.

That's what is meant by being dialed in.

When you are dialed in, you can feel every twitch of the bait. You can sense every change in texture on the bottom. When you make a cast, you can almost see the three-pounder moving in on the bait. You know he is about to inhale it even before he strikes.

My greatest moments in fishing have come when I was dialed in.

I was fishing a Classic on the James River near Richmond and had been having a so-so week. It was the final day and I was catching fish. But I needed bigger fish to move up in the standings.

It was almost time for weigh-in. I was on plane racing out of a creek. There were thousands of little inlets, little washes; they are everywhere on that part of the river. Running by one of those thousands of little fingers, I suddenly had a feeling: *I need to fish this.*

I spun the boat around, fired a cast on the spot, and caught a three-pounder.

Then I was out of there.

I knew I was dialed in. The air was crisper and cleaner, and the sky was bluer—and all my senses were operating at the highest level. I could see farther and hear better. But most of all, I could *feel* things and I could *hear* things.

I heard that voice again as I approached the riprap at the

mouth of the basin where check-in was being held. I had four minutes until I had to check in with the tournament director. I threw a crank bait toward the riprap, and while it was still in the air, I knew with 100 percent certainty I was going to catch a bass.

The bait hit the water.

I started reeling. The bait did not move ten feet before a bass ate it.

Those two fish jumped me from 20th in the tournament up to 11th.

When you are dialed in, magic is commonplace.

Not only do you come to accept it, you expect it.

An angler who is dialed in knows when to stop fishing in one place and when to go to another. He knows how to make choices and decisions that have nothing to do with conscious thought. It is all unconscious. It's not seeing a laydown or a bush and saying, "I bet a fish is in there." It is the feeling and the knowledge, the sure and certain knowledge that *I will catch one.*

It is not a science. It is all feeling.

THE BASS

~

In the past few years, bass fishing has become more of a national sport.

But bass fishing today is like the space program in the fifties. We know a lot, we've talked about it forever, the technology is there, we just haven't mastered it.

No one catches bass every time he goes on the water. The bass may not be very smart, but he is smart enough to keep us from catching him all the time. No one figures them out every time. Rick Clunn has won the Classic four times. He holds the

Classic record of 21 bass weighing in at 75 pounds 9 ounces—a record that may never be broken. You can fish with Rick Clunn and learn more in a day about bass fishing than you could learn in a year on your own.

But Rick Clunn still gets beat by the bass from time to time.

B.A.S.S. has more than 600,000 members and 40 percent of those members, or some 240,000 anglers, have computers with CD-ROM drives that they use to study lakes and rivers and everything ever put on a CD about bass. Plus they have numerous pages on the Web to research the bass. All this technology notwithstanding, they get beat by the fish from time to time.

It is this wild card element that brings the magic to bass fishing. Here's another example.

In 1995, David Fritts was the top man in bassdom. He caught so many fish that when he started casting, it was called a Fritts Blitz. In one tournament on Lake Seminolein, he had a 13-pound lead going into the final day. All the media were talking about another Fritts Blitz.

At weigh-in on the last day, the crowd was stunned.

David Fritts came to the scales with an empty bag. He got skunked. He got zip. Not a single fish.

It was as if Tiger Woods failed to break a hundred. It was as if Michael Jordan had a game where he couldn't make a single point. It was as if Jeff Gordon couldn't drive faster than 40 miles an hour.

The drama was heightened when Claude Fishburne, an angler who had been trying for eight years to win a tournament, had an incredible day on the water and came in first. Claude, whom we call Fish, won his second tournament a few days later. After eight dry years, Fish won more than $170,000 in about 30 days.

Bass fishing is magic.

Rods and reels have advanced technologically far beyond what they were when I began my career. So has fishing line. Occasionally a new bait comes along, but baits are so varied and so thought-out that many of the new ones are more gimmickry than anything else. There's not much more you can do with motors except boost the horsepower, and we don't need that. Fish finders, depth finders, and GPS, which were unknown to fishermen just a few years ago, are commonplace on the trail. Dozens of us pros are out there every year teaching hundreds of seminars. Books and magazines and newspaper columnists have revealed, so it would seem, every possible secret and technique for catching the bass. If you stop to think about the people involved, the money involved, the technology, the horsepower, and the brainpower devoted to catching this one green fish, it is a worldwide phenomenon of staggering proportions.

Yet no matter how great our knowledge and how sophisticated our equipment, no matter how much we read or how much we learn, sometimes the bass still wins.

MORNING

∼

Early morning is my favorite time on the water.

Sometimes the fog is so thick, you can see only ten feet beyond the bow. The water is flat and dark. Then the sun begins burning through, and little swirls of fog begin dancing. I look toward the rising sun and see the fog beginning to cook on the flat skillet of the lake.

The shadows become long and the morning light is tinged with pink and orange. An osprey takes off from his nest in a big oak and climbs toward the sun.

And then, far out on the very edge of my vision, is the distinctive silhouette of another bass boat, low in the water; a big 200hp engine on the stern, a small seat sticking up on the aft deck. And there on the bow is the angler, leaning forward in intense concentration, his foot on the trolling motor, backlit by the morning sun.

He is bent over studying his sonar. Then he lifts his eyes to study the water, to squint at a fallen tree and a distant grass line. Shad suddenly skitter across the surface like a handful of silver dollars. They twist and dart and leap in the early sunlight.

With each cast the angler makes, a tiny explosion of mist pops from his reel and hangs suspended a few seconds, a million glittering points of light sparkling in the soft morning air, hanging over his hands, giving give him the air of a magician performing a secret ritual.

His line arcs through the air in a perfect cast, and the sun illuminates it and turns it into a white-hot thread.

He is leaning forward, seeing nothing but the water, feeling the bait and sensing in his hands and in his heart that Mr. Bass is down there and on the prowl, searching, and about to eat his bait.

He is ready.

He is doing what so few people in today's world are fortunate enough to do...he is living his dream.

He is a figure of magic.

He is hope.

He is America.

ACKNOWLEDGEMENTS

~

Throughout life there are many people who touch our lives and help create who we are. I would like to thank some of these special people in my life.

Mom—for the values and beliefs, always being there and helping out, and for all the special love only a mother can give.

Polly—for everything, my lifelong partner, and for the support and love that allows me to live my dream.

Amy and Shaw-Shaw—for not complaining when I am traveling and for being terrific kids.

Susan and Stewart Powers—for always helping me grow and for introducing me to the love of my life.

Mary, Ernie, Scott, and Andy Fivecoat—for keeping everything running.

Jack and Noranell Heroman—for a home away from home and for all the crawfish I can eat.

Tim Tucker—for your guidance and friendship.

Gerry Bevis—for making me a better fisherman and for being a lifelong friend.

Larry Lazoen—for your sincere friendship.

Dr. George Benchimol—thanks for keeping me running.

Tommy and Pat Clark—for allowing me to be a part of the HP Hook.

Bobby Reddish—for having such a great work ethic and for allowing me to fish those early years.

Robert Ives—for always being there and helping out.

Ironwood and everyone on the television crew of *"One More Cast With Shaw Grigsby"*— for putting up with me.

Calvin Johnson—for all the neat stuff and the secret baits.

Captains Al Dopirak and Steve Kilpatrick—for the fun times.

Doug Hannon—a special friend who always keeps me thinking and makes me laugh.

Joe Smith and Terry Heist—for always being there to fix whatever I break and for being the best service crew.

Jeff Miller and all the gang at Miller's Boating Center—for all you do.

Rick Clunn—for being an inspiration off the water as well as on.

Gary Klein and Paul Elias—for being great teammates and friends.

Guido Hibdon—for being one of my fishing teachers.

My sponsors past and present—without their help I would not be able to compete.

The fans—without you this sport would not be what it is and neither would I.

Dr. Bob Reinert—for the details.

Ann Lewis—a special thanks, without whom this book would never have come about.

Ray Scott and B.A.S.S.—for creating the competitive sport of bass fishing.

Terry Chupp—for his unwavering dedication.

Robert Coram—for your patience and diligence.

And most importantly, Jesus Christ, through whom all things are possible.